STORY

The Power
of Narrative
for Christian
Leaders

By
Jay R. Martinson

BEACON HILL PRESS
OF KANSAS CITY

978-0-8341-3549-9

Printed in the
United States of America

Cover design: Sherwin Schwarztrock
Interior design: Sharon Page

Library of Congress Cataloging-in-Publication Data

Martinson, Jay, 1964-
  Story : the power of narrative for Christian leaders / by Jay Martinson.
    pages cm
  Includes bibliographical references.
  ISBN 978-0-8341-3549-9 (pbk. : alk. paper) 1. Storytelling—Religious aspects—
Christianity. 2. Christian leadership. I. Title.
  BT83.78.M35 2016
  248.4'6—dc23
                          2015026962

All Scripture quotations, unless indicated, are taken from *The Holy Bible: New International Version®* (NIV®). Copyright © 1973, 1978, 1984, 2011 by Biblica, Inc.™ Used by
permission of Zondervan. All rights reserved worldwide. *www.zondervan.com.*

Scripture quotations marked (KJV) are taken from *The Holy Bible: King James Version.*

The internet addresses, email addresses, and phone numbers in this book are
accurate at the time of publication. They are provided as a resource. Beacon Hill
Press does not endorse them or vouch for their content or permanence.

10 9 8 7 6 5 4 3 2 1

Acknowledgments

Thanks, Mom and Dad, for leading me onto my own faith journey and for your constant, unconditional support. Thanks, Rachel, Andrew, T.J., Tamera, Lucy, Tad, Dawson, Jonah, Beckett, and Leona for the endless source of joy and stories you've given me. Most of all, thanks, Jeanette, for writing me a storied marriage.

Contents

Introduction

In the 2000 film *Remember the Titans*, Coach Boone, played by Denzel Washington, is faced with the enormous challenge of uniting his racially divided high school football team in Alexandria, Virginia, during the early 1970s. In one of the movie's more poignant scenes, Coach Boone allows the team to stop in the middle of an intense jog in the early morning fog. Still breathing hard, bent over with hands on their knees, they peer upward at their coach. Boone gestures at the dew-filled, rolling fields surrounding them and delivers this monologue:

Anybody know what this place is? This is Gettysburg. This is where they fought the Battle of Gettysburg. Fifty thousand men died right here on this field, fighting the same fight that we're still fighting amongst ourselves today. This green field right here was painted red, bubbling with the blood of young boys—smoke and hot lead pouring right through their bodies. Listen to their souls, men.

"I killed my brother with malice in my heart."

"Hatred destroyed my family."

You listen and take a lesson from the dead. If we don't come together right now, on this hallowed ground, we too will be destroyed, just like they were.

I don't care if you don't like each other or not, but you will respect each other. And maybe, I don't know, maybe we'll learn to play this game like men.

Coach Boone is painfully aware of the situation he faces. His young men are divided, yet a divided team cannot win games. He could threaten them, tell them to get with it or lose their spots on the team. He could send a memo detailing the benefits of racial integration. He could lecture, scold, demand, or plea. If set in our modern era, he might tweet an ultimatum, give a multi-slide PowerPoint, or perhaps send a group text, saying, "Get w/ it or u r outta here n don't b L8!"

Instead, Coach Boone chooses to tell a *story*.

Once Upon a Story

We are narrative beings. Before Twitter and e-readers, before movies and radio dramas, before the printing press and written languages, there were stories. The media through which we tell them continue to evolve, but our storytelling nature remains the same. It remains an essential aspect of what it means to be human.

You probably don't remember your own baby shower, but it's likely your mother received classic children's books. From birth onward, you probably heard fairy tales, fables, and perhaps even some original bedtime stories told by especially creative parents.

With the aid of flannelgraphs and other media, we learned the Bible through the telling of amazing stories. Who can forget the image of a man living inside the belly of a whale? As a child, I used to imagine Jonah huddled around a small campfire inside the massive rib cage. I'm not sure why I assumed the whale's belly was akin to a dimly lit cave containing wood and matches.

In school, our learning likewise took place using stories. From stories told by our textbooks and our teachers, we learned the virtues of our culture and the American spirit. Remember the cherry tree? A kite, a key, and a lightning bolt? Three sailing ships? The Alamo? A lantern in a Boston church? A tea party? A pilgrim feast? A woman's refusal to move to the back of a bus? Even the most abstract of subjects—math— was often taught through *story* problems.

At home, our parents taught life lessons through stories. Before receiving the car keys on a winter day, we first needed to hear Mom's story about the time she was a teenage driver and experienced black ice on a country road. Before we quit the sports team, Dad told us a story that made us reconsider. Applying for college? Mom told a story. Going on a first date? Mom, Dad, brother, sister, and even Uncle Billy offered (usually unsolicited!) stories. First breakup? An avalanche of stories designed to make us feel better.

The average American will spend nearly five hours a day watching television and view eight movies per year at the theater, not to mention the time spent viewing movies streamed on our computers and mobile devices. We are drawn to stories. These mediated stories engage our minds for entertainment, vicarious escape into other experiences, inspiration, education, and cathartic emotional release.

Stories Stick

Ancient Greeks like Aristotle and Plato used the power of story and myth as tools to engage audiences. A few hundred years later, another teacher named Jesus did the same thing. In parable stories, Jesus taught profound concepts. Listeners might have walked away unmoved from an abstract sermon about principles. They couldn't leave a story, however, that connected these principles to the stuff of their own lives: farming, raising children, and working for unfair bosses.

Mere abstract statements of policy might leave us. Stories don't. From the stories, we derive and create meaning. The lessons finally become real. Clichés become connections. *Stories stick*. Stories become integral lenses through which we come to understand our own life experiences. These experiences then become our *own* stories—a repository of powerful lenses, only a thought away when we need them.

From cradle to grave, stories infuse meaning into our lives. They entertain, teach, inspire, comfort, and confront. Before there were multimedia platforms for transmitting them, stories were simply told orally from one to another, as a mother to a child, or a speaker to a small crowd gathered in the shade of a tree. Modern life has changed how we tell stories, but the centrality of story in our lives remains the same.

Narratives have the power to do far more than merely entertain and teach. They can inspire us to change our lives. Stories are not merely things we read, hear, or watch. Stories are things we live. We understand and express our lives narratively. We tell stories about the events of our day. On a larger scale, we can also tell our life stories. We all think narratively, regardless of age, education, intellect, or socioeconomic status. Our stories define who we are.

□   □   □

As believers, we take the Great Commission seriously. We hold the greatest truth in these ordinary clay pots of our lives and yearn to share it with all. We want to reach our children, friends, neighbors, and world for Christ. As faith leaders, our goal is so much more than simply being kind, providing our churches as safe places for quality programming, inspirational speaking, and family-friendly activities. We leaders sense the urgency and gravity of the call of Christ. We want to make a difference for the kingdom. We *want to lead.*

We know that leadership requires a foundation of integrity and character. We know that the Lord calls us to serve. We know that effective leadership requires a variety of functional skills that include planning, organization, collaboration, and delegation. However, leadership also involves communication—the vehicle through which we connect with others. Our message is lost unless we can express it. Our vision is trapped in our minds unless we can vividly connect it to the minds and hearts of others. Our love and compassion are often expressed through our actions, but distinguishing the love and compassion inspired by Jesus Christ from mere kindhearted benevolence requires *language.*

To lead effectively, I must be willing to step up and engage others—individuals and audiences alike. My personality and style will differ from yours. You may be charismatic while I might not. You may use humor naturally while I might not. You might be able to quote enormous amounts of Scripture and scholarly writing while I might not. You might be a formally trained pastor, having mastered an inductive homiletic style, while I may have no formal training. The great news is that God can and wants to use us all. We need to communicate from our individual personalities, styles, and training.

Regardless of our differences, however, we leaders all have one thing in common, and it's the exact same thing those we lead have in common—*the story*. Fred Craddock reminds us that "stories are not decorative embroidering on the gospel... One does well as a storyteller when reaching the point wherein the story carries the gospel, like seed carries its future in its own bosom."[1]

To change one's narrative is to change one's very identity. This applies to one's faith identity as much as any other. Changes can be radical—as in, a conversion experience—but they can also represent smaller instances of growth. How do we challenge people to change the faith narratives they have for their lives? You guessed it: We engage their individual narratives through the power of narrative. And that is what the term *storied leadership*, which will appear throughout the book, refers to.

SECTION ONE

THE STORY OF STORY

For a man, proposing marriage these days is not as simple as it used to be. He cannot simply drop to one knee and present an open box bearing a ring. Nope. There's no story there. We men are realizing that women not only want the ring; they also want the story. Their girlfriends will want to hear all about the proposal and will undoubtedly ask, *"How* did he propose?" And there had better be a good story to offer. That story not only has to satisfy the contemporary audience; it also must be built to last a lifetime! It will need to bring smiles to faces of children who ask, "How did Dad propose to you, Mom?" In essence, they are asking, *How did this story begin?*

Once upon a time.

In the beginning.

Here's how it all started.

These sentences are all familiar to us because every story needs a beginning. Even a book *about* story needs a beginning. Before delving into types of stories and ways to tell stories well, we need to step back and answer a few questions regarding how this all began.

Why are we focusing on story?

How is story connected to leadership?

With so many ways of communicating the gospel these days, why place so much emphasis on narrative?

So, to begin, let's answer these questions about the story, of story.

1   Story as Leadership

A traveler made his way along a road. The North Wind and the Sun wagered a challenge: Which of them could make the man remove his coat? In this fable by Aesop, the harder the North Wind blew, the tighter the traveler wrapped his coat around himself. When the Sun shone, however, its warmth inspired the man to remove his coat.

Orders, commands, debate, and forceful arguments are necessary forms of communication. They are also legitimate forms of motivation in particular forms of leadership. They are not, however, typically effective for communicating gospel truths. Like the traveler with his coat, many of us pull our defenses tighter around ourselves when we are pushed. Personal stories, however, tend to engage and draw listeners in. Like the sun, they *inspire* an openness toward change rather than demand it. When it comes to communicating gospel truths, we should be the sun.

My intent with this book is simple. I want to encourage you to use the power of story to lead others in their faith journeys. So it's about story. It's about narrative. It's about communication. It's about evangelism. It's about leadership. But before getting too far, we need some simple definitions.

Story: A factual or fictional account of events. The word *story* becomes interesting when we precede it with adjectives. Tragic story.

Funny story. Fascinating story. My story. Her story. The gospel story. Stories give structure to our human experience. They allow us to understand events that happened in the past; they give us a grammar for understanding what is happening to us right now; and they allow us to plan and choose events we want for our future.

Narrative: The telling or writing of a story. The ways we tell stories, or the events of our lives, are never objective. The telling of our stories reflects how we see the world, ourselves, and others. On what do we focus and elaborate? What do we ignore and minimize? Even our greatest attempts to tell stories objectively are filtered through choices. We are not merely storytellers; we are story editors. Our understanding of reality is in part based on which narratives we accept as true: those we've heard, those we've told, and those we believe about ourselves.

Communication: The process of exchanging ideas among minds through words, symbols, and behaviors, both intentionally and unintentionally. Communication is one of those things that is difficult to define, but we all know when it isn't being done well. Successful communicators realize the complexity of the concept and, like an artist, can choose among the various media available to express a particular thought to a particular person or group.

Evangelism: Intentional actions designed to encourage others toward a stronger relationship with Christ. As such, this includes sharing the gospel with one who has never heard it. It also includes the encouragement for spiritual growth at any point along another's faith journey. It can happen person to person, person to group, or even group to group (as in, a church sending evangelistic messages directed to a community).

Leadership: The intentional act of guiding or influencing others for their well-being. This definition does not consider coercion or manipulation to be leadership, although these things do serve to guide and influence—just not for another's well-being. This definition also does not imply a particular position or title. *Anyone can lead.*

☐ ☐ ☐

Since you are reading this book, I'm making some assumptions about you. I assume you are interested in encouraging others to a closer walk with Christ (i.e., evangelism) and are open to finding effective ways of doing so (i.e., communication). Your desire to influence people for their well-being makes you a leader. This book is designed to help you lead, communicate, and evangelize using the power of story—hence, to develop your storied leadership.

Reflect or Discuss

1. How does the fable of the North Wind and the Sun relate to how you prefer to be led? Recall examples of when you've experienced both styles.

2. Given the definition of leadership used in this book, to what degree do you see yourself as a leader?

3. Although most of us have been communicating since before we could walk (or even talk!), why is it that nobody has ever perfected it and misunderstandings remain so common?

4. While the word *evangelism* brings forth a variety of images in our minds, how does the definition this book provides pertain to your own goals?

2   The Power of Story

"What's in a name? That which we call a rose,
by any other name would smell as sweet."
—William Shakespeare, *Romeo and Juliet*

Naming

Romeo and Juliet's love is passionate and real. In today's language, Romeo would likely call Juliet his soul mate. There's just one problem, though—their last names. The Montagues and Capulets are warring families, so it is impossible for a Montague son and a Capulet daughter to break ranks from the family feud. In one of the most famous lines from Shakespeare, Juliet ponders the power of naming. *It's just a name; what's the big deal?* she seems to demand. The problem is that names and naming are indeed very big deals.

Upon creating the world, God's first recorded actions involve naming creation. God then empowers Adam to join in this naming process. Significant life changes in the Bible are often marked by name changes. Abram to Abraham. Sarai to Sarah. Jacob to Israel. Simon to Peter. Saul to Paul. We use language to reflect and communicate changes in identity.

Recently a friend excitedly told me that God had provided an enormous answer to prayer: Their physician formally diagnosed their son with Asperger's syndrome. Does this sound like an answered prayer to you? It was for him. Finally he and his wife had a name, a label, a definition for their son's behavioral challenges. Receiving the diagnosis didn't provide a cure, but it did provide perspective. All the random symptoms suddenly made sense and had order. Directions for moving ahead with therapy and treatment were now clear.

Naming, labeling, and definitions don't control events; they give structure to our thoughts. If leadership is guiding or influencing others for their well-being, one powerful way to do so is through naming, labeling, and defining.

The narrative telling of our stories is an act of naming. The stories we tell, and the way we tell them, give definition to our experiences. The details we include—areas of focus and areas of omission—all essentially define that experience. And two people seldom define one experience in the same way. Police reports often demonstrate this truth: Four people witnessing the same crime may offer different descriptions of a criminal's height, clothing, race, getaway car, and actions. These differences exist due to the witnesses' standpoints, perspectives, perceptions, expectations, beliefs, and biases.

My friends Beth and Kevin once returned from winter vacation to find that the pipes in their house had burst, resulting in more than $100,000 of damage to their historic home. When *I* tell this story, it sounds like a tragedy. Plaster was destroyed, wiring was compromised, every appliance was broken, and layers of ice destroyed hardwood flooring. Their version of the story, however, is different: They got new floors, new plumbing, new appliances, and a new furnace, all paid for by the insurance company.

It is important for leaders to understand that we can have multiple narratives for the same sets of events.

How can I challenge the narrative of a person who sees no hope? How can my church's social media offer a consistent narrative of God's grace changing lives in our community when local news narratives focus largely on despair? How can I use the power of narrative to inspire change and correction? Forgiveness? Hope? Reconciliation? How can I enter the lives of my children and grandchildren to illustrate a Christ-centered narrative?

The moment we utter words, we are urging people to look at the world in a particular manner. To rhetorician Richard Weaver, this is referred to as the sermonic nature of language. Whether it is intentional, language becomes a vehicle of influence to see and understand life from our own perspectives. Rhetoric—or, the art of using language—always presents us with the opportunity to choose. Whether we choose nobly or otherwise is up to us. Weaver somberly reminds us that, "since all utterance influences us in one or the other of these directions, it is important that the direction be the right one."[1]

□ □ □

I had just gotten my sleeping bag zipped up and my head on the tiny camping pillow. The flickering light of the dying campfire projected it onto the side of our nylon tent. The shadowy image grew larger as it drew closer. Suddenly, claws stabbed into my unprotected dwelling to reveal the glaring eyes—and sharp teeth—of a grizzly bear!

Stories like this have been told for many years as a favorite feature called "This Happened to Me" in *Outdoor Life* magazine. Although we love stories, we especially love true stories. True stories enable us to identify with the protagonists. We experience vicariously what they experience. We can challenge or doubt the credibility of theories and abstract claims, for example, that grizzly bears may slice through a tent. *Says who? How do you know they will?* Firsthand stories contain inherent authority. Ungrounded claims can be questioned. But stories just *are*. Their proof lies in the credibility of the speaker. If we trust the speaker, we believe the story. As Christians, we sometimes worry we won't have enough knowledge, enough answers, enough evidence. While we should seek to expand our theological knowledge, our strongest proof often lies in our own stories.

Oral Testimony

When John Wesley began to articulate the doctrine of Christian perfection, or sanctification, he did not rely merely upon intellectual reasoning, philosophical syllogisms, or natural laws. Instead, it was through the personal testimonies of religious experience offered by people with whom Wesley came into contact. This "continuing and consistent evidence of experience"[2] helped him solidify his doctrine. These testimonies were in the form of personal, narrative accounts that essentially communicated, *This is what happened to me.*

Oral testimonies held at least two important functions in the early church (and still do today), the first being faith attainment. John Wesley admitted to Moravian Peter Böhler his uncertainty of preaching until he became certain of his own faith. Böhler told him to "preach faith until you have it."[3] The act of publicly verbalizing his faith to others was presented to Wesley as a faith-creating as well as faith-sustaining act. Phoebe Palmer, an outspoken advocate for the doctrine of sanctification during the nineteenth century, assigned a similar function to testimonies. Since Christ had already provided the means for sanctification, all the seeker had to do was claim the experience. Public testimony served to solidify the experience.

The other function of testimonies involves that of faith maintenance. In accordance with the views of Wesley, Palmer, and later holiness leaders, testimonies shared within the context of small groups have been an important feature of faith maintenance. The oral sharing of individual testimonies, or faith stories, were regular parts of Bible study groups led by John and Charles Wesley at Oxford. At Tuesday Meetings for the Promotion of Holiness at Palmer's home, those in attendance were expected to give updates of the spiritual condition of their souls. Revivals (or camp meetings) became a champion for the promotion of the holiness doctrine. Following singing, a sermon, and an altar call, revival services could continue well into the night with the sharing of testimonies. Many contemporary holiness churches maintain a similar emphasis on sharing personal testimonies.

The power of oral testimonies is enormous. They are important for unbelieving listeners who may see themselves in the stories and feel likewise drawn toward the Lord. They are important for storytellers, to ascribe narrative to their experiences: *This is what God did for me.* While testimonies are about the work of the Lord, they also frequently give credit to those who led us toward God in the first place. As such, they encourage all believers to continue reaching out. As an example, Dr. Woody Webb, the vice president of student development at Olivet Nazarene University, offers his testimony:

My growing-up years were spent in the small town of Marion, Illinois, with five brothers and sisters. I was raised in a home where church was never a priority, and my parents worked hard to provide care and keep the family together.

As a young boy, I was often prayed over by a grandmother who was a wonderful Christian example and a charter member of the Church of the Nazarene. On rare occasions, some of my siblings and I attended vacation Bible school or the occasional special program at the local Nazarene church where my grandmother went. Those days ceased following her unexpected death. As far as I knew, my churchgoing days were over.

Little did I know that my grandmother's prayers would be answered about the time I entered the ninth grade. A substitute teacher named Mrs. Lee pulled me aside after class one day and asked me why I had not been to church. As the wife of the new Nazarene pastor, she recalled seeing my name on the Sunday school roll of that tiny Nazarene church. Her invitation and follow-up convinced me to give it another try; after all, how could I say no to a teacher?

One Sunday, then two, then three, and before long it was a habit. It wasn't too many weeks before I knelt at the church altar and Pastor Lee and others prayed with me, and I accepted Christ as my personal Savior.

The months passed, and I continued to grow in my faith. I can't tell you how many pounds of ham and cheese sandwiches I consumed as I sat around Pastor and Mrs. Lee's dining room table most Sunday nights after church. Their example taught me what it meant to serve the Lord.

Over the next few months, I began to sense a call into full-time Christian ministry, and Pastor Lee began to talk to me about preparing for that call at a place called Olivet Nazarene College. In the fall of 1982, I enrolled as a freshman religion major living in Chapman Hall.

My years as a student at Olivet were marked by tremendous spiritual growth. And, by God's grace and the support of others, I completed my master's degree in 1988.

Rev. and Mrs. Lee continued pastoring that church in Marion for many years and had the privilege of leading both my parents into a saving relationship with Jesus Christ.

I've often wondered, what if I had skipped school that day Mrs. Lee pulled me aside after class? Or what if she hadn't risked pulling me aside at all? Or what if I had ignored her invitation? What if...?

The narrative telling (and retelling) of stories has power. Our narratives name, label, and define the events of our lives. How we choose to tell our stories is sermonic in that language is never value-neutral. When describing any event, we engage in leadership by influencing others. Our narratives influence ourselves and others through what aspects of a story we include and elaborate on as well by what we omit or minimize. Narratives also influence by the rhetorical style, form, and arrangement we artfully employ in their telling. While these principles of power apply to messages within all stories, they are most important to those of us wanting to share the gospel story.

Reflect or Discuss

1. The author suggests that naming has power. How have name choices, name-calling, and name changes proven this to be true in your life?

2. Recall an instance when you heard a story that seemed hard to believe, but your trust in the storyteller was enough proof for its authenticity?

3. How have others' testimonies affected (and how do they continue to affect) your own faith?

4. How have others been affected by your testimony?

5. If you are reluctant to share your testimony, why is that the case?

3 Our Narrative DNA

When my father and his sister Marlene start telling childhood stories about growing up in Minnesota, I hear about fishing and a variety of pets: horses, dogs, cats, raccoons, and the occasional bear cub. But one type of story that seems to surface frequently concerns the *journeys* my dad took. Don't get the wrong idea here; these weren't exactly international trips. In fact, they seldom involved leaving their modest-sized yard. But to a kid, a yard may as well be the entire world. So my dad didn't exactly discover new territories or exotic species. But as the old screen door slammed behind him, he knew he was heading out for a new journey, answering the call of wanderlust.

Many of us are drawn to leave the familiar, the comfortable, and the status quo to experience something else, something *greater*—a true journey! Sure, we seek changes of landscape and scenery, but we also seek changes of *identity*. There is a growing industry devoted to providing experiences for those who can afford them. These experiences include remote African safaris, Colorado dude ranches, wilderness exploration, Canadian canoe fishing trips, mountain climbing expeditions, and—most recently—even space travel. Very often, work-and-witness trips function in this way for many Christians. We are drawn to give of ourselves to help others, but we are equally captivated by the idea of leaving our comfort zones to experience the unknown and return—*changed*—with a new story to tell.

Whether we have the courage (and the currency) required to embark on such journeys, we can enjoy them vicariously. Think of the plots of the last year's top-grossing movies. How many of them represent some kind of journey for the protagonist? These journeys may be physical, emotional, social, even spiritual. Whether eating outrageously priced popcorn at the theater or spilling microwaved kernels between the cushions of our own recliners, we take the journey too. We identify with the protagonist on his journey to prove himself innocent of a crime. We cheer for the athlete in arduous training for a race nobody thinks she can win. We wince and groan along with the prisoner of war as he receives lashes from his prison guard after a failed attempt to escape.

You're So Dramatic

Nearly every story—from Hollywood blockbusters to our three-minute water cooler stories—follows what has come to be called the basic dramatic structure. A rudimentary diagram of dramatic structure (sometimes called Freytag's pyramid) illustrates how most stories are structured.

Most stories begin with **exposition**, or details of the setting (time, place, characters, etc.). Then a plot is introduced that offers **rising action**. This could be the growing argument between a teenager and a parent, a threat to turn a park into a parking lot, and so on. The rising action builds to a point of **climax**, where the growing tensions collide and actions are taken. After the climax comes the **falling action**, where things slowly begin to sort themselves out, where they finally come to rest in the *dénouement*, which is the French word for "resolution." The resolution could be a happy ending where everything works out and characters are at peace. Or, alternatively, *dénouement* could be the realization that things will never change, or the acceptance of inevitable tragedy.

As natural storytellers, we expect stories to follow this basic structure. Less obvious, however, is that we also tend to view our own lives through the lens of this same dramatic structure.

When our daughter Rachel was a teenager, we ordered her an iPod. At that time, Apple offered the option of free engraving. There was really only enough space for the equivalent of one short sentence, so I considered multiple things that might really capture her spirit. Soon, an obvious answer presented itself to me. It read: *I've got a story…*

Seemingly every time she entered a room, Rachel's first words were, "I've got a story." She'd offer a narrative from her day, something funny that happened at swim practice, something outrageous a teacher said, or one of the many embarrassing things that seemed to happen to her on a regular basis. She still entertains us (and hundreds more, in status updates on Facebook) with these stories that have now expanded to include the crazy antics of her husband and three sons.

Regardless of her stories' themes, they typically followed the basic dramatic structure. She offered some quick exposition: "I was at swim practice this morning, and Coach had us swimming 500 meters." It then had some rising action: "I was thinking that this was about my best time ever as I was passing up other girls." Then the climax: "…when all of a sudden I lost track of where I was and rammed my head right into the wall!" Then she ended with the falling action and dénouement: "But then somehow I regained my senses and finished the race—dead last." Nearly all stories—even the little stories of our ordinary days—follow this basic story structure. And when someone's story doesn't follow this structure, we are left confused. We wonder things like, *Is this story going somewhere?* when the storyteller doesn't offer rising action.

What if Rachel had only told us that she was swimming fast? That might have been the point of her story, but we'd likely be waiting to hear if there was some other action or place she was going with it. If she told us that she hit her head hard and then ended the story there, that would be equally incomplete and leave us asking things like, "Were you okay? Did you have to get out of the pool? What did you do next?" Storytellers owe us a sense of closure; we don't want to be left hanging.

The reason we are drawn to stories, view our lives in terms of stories, and even interpret what happens to us following the basic dramatic structure for stories is not because of a Hollywood conspiracy or subtle attempt to brainwash us. Rather, it seems Hollywood producers simply generate stories that reflect how we've been experiencing our lives for thousands of years. Certainly the kinds of stories we consume also serve to reinforce this narrative mindset. Not only do we tend to interpret our lives through this basic narrative lens; we also tend to view our lives themselves as narrative journeys.

The Monomyth

In his classic book *Hero with a Thousand Faces*, Joseph Campbell explains the human tendency to view our lives as journeys. Keep in mind that Campbell was not a Christian; this fact makes his findings all the more interesting. Campbell was a noted American mythologist who felt driven to understand the human experience. He studied stories from across the globe, ancient and contemporary alike. His conclusion was fairly simple yet powerful: Human beings are captivated and driven by the "hero's journey." Regardless of the particular culture, Campbell found that many of our most popular and enduring stories follow a highly predictable pattern. He called this the hero's journey, or, the Monomyth, because it was a singular story pattern resonating across all cultures.[1]

Although the hero's journey can take various forms with unique twists and turns, Campbell discovered that most of these stories follow a cyclical thematic pattern. It begins with experiencing a call to adventure. It could be an urging from a friend, a selection (young shepherd David being selected from the pasture), stepping up to protect a loved one (Katniss Everdeen from *The Hunger Games* trilogy), or even finding oneself accidentally thrust into a journey by some strange set of events (Dorothy in *The Wizard of Oz*).

After some reluctance, the hero embarks on the journey, often receiving some kind of aid from helpers or mentors along the way (David has Jonathan, Katniss has Haymitch, Dorothy has her companions). Leaving the world of comfort, the hero faces uncertainties, trials, and temptations that allow the hero the opportunity to strengthen his or her character. David faces Goliath, Katniss faces the Hunger Games and the forces of the Capitol, and Dorothy faces the Wicked Witch of the West.

The climax of the journey, according to Campbell, is an encounter with a higher being (David depends on the Lord, Katniss becomes the Mockingjay at the request of President Coin, and Dorothy meets the almighty wizard). Further, they often receive what Campbell calls the ultimate boon—some new power, ability, or confidence (David becomes king, Katniss receives specialized weapons, and Dorothy receives ruby slippers).

Although the journey has been difficult, the return to the hero's normal life presents an equal challenge because the old self is gone, and one has to integrate back into one's world as a transformed person. It could be a new character formed out of adversity (David's eventual legacy of being one after God's own heart), a new status or position (Katniss as the Mockingjay—the symbol of the rebellion), or a new perspective or realization (Dorothy's newfound appreciation for home). For Campbell, the final stage of the journey represents a state of freedom. Having survived one's fears, one finds a place of peace and freedom and renewed appreciation for life.

Campbell does not suggest that every narrative in every culture since the dawn of time follows these steps precisely. But the presence of this nearly universal narrative suggests that this basic structure resonates well with our human experience. Something sparks within us a sense of discontent; we want something more. There's something missing in our lives; we feel incomplete. We seek for it while at the same time feeling some reluctance (perhaps pressure from friends and loved ones not to venture out). Yet we still feel compelled to seek that which we sense is missing in our lives.

Doesn't this narrative—which Campbell suggests is universal—ultimately represent the seeking of our Savior? It took Campbell a lifetime to articulate in an academic sense what many Christians already know or believe: *We are all born seeking the Savior.* Metaphorically, Campbell's Monomyth is our basic narrative DNA—a rather simple realization that can have enormous implications for how we attempt to communicate the gospel.

Star of the Show

This universal notion of the hero's journey makes sense. Our search for someone or something to heroically complete our incompleteness rings true with what we've all observed in human nature. But there's a problem. Sensing our incompleteness, we bravely (even heroically) set out on our journey to find that which will save us—our ultimate hero. But whom will we cast in the role of our hero?

We hold fairly open auditions. Who shows up wanting the part? Alcohol and other mind-altering drugs deliver stunning auditions that promise us satisfaction. Personal accomplishments, wealth, success, and affirmation impressively stick to the script that performance brings happiness. Human relationships (and our total dependence upon them) offer Oscar-winning performances—starring friends, pastors, spouses, our children, and even extramarital affairs.

These open auditions are flooded with many who promise to repair that which we find broken in our lives. But the one who wins the Academy Award is (drumroll, please, as we open the envelope): *ourselves*. As Campbell observed, the person venturing forth—the main character—is ultimately on a journey toward *becoming* the hero. The main character is not a hero yet. The idea of the main character becoming a hero is still an attractive myth in literature, but it doesn't work in real life. We ultimately tend to cast ourselves as hero of our own lives, which makes sense. *I may not be perfect, but at least I'm used to working with myself.* Right?

The big "so what?" seems simple enough: We are born seeking a savior. But in the narrative of our lives, we often cast ourselves in the savior role. That way, we can draw on any number of our highly willing understudies (accomplishments, substances, relationships, addictions, etc.) to perform in this role on a given day. The problem here is obvious to believers: We can't cast ourselves in the role of hero. We're not superheroes, and we're not saviors. With myself in the role of hero, I can only mess up my life—and badly. Sadly, many stop this hero's journey short. Instead of simply searching for the Creator, we cast ourselves as hero. Our journey then begins, and ends, with *ourselves*. We're no longer just the people with the problems; we also see ourselves as the ones who are able to fix them.

Connecting the Dots

Virtually every narrative across cultures, from the earliest recorded tales (including the Bible), is a variation of humans facing conflict (rising action) that seeks climax and resolution. Further, they reflect ordinary people entering the classic hero's journey to find some ultimate atonement. Why do these themes prevail across time and culture? Why do these connect with all of us? Maybe this is precisely how our Creator made us. Perhaps God created us with a sense of incompleteness, a wanting, a need that can only be filled by God. In our own various ways, we enter into journeys trying to fill that need with something more.

Unique to humanity is the ability for self-reflection. We can view the events of our lives (our stories) and express them as narratives to others and to ourselves, reflecting our interpretation of those events. As an act of naming and defining, choosing a narrative has enormous power for, and over, us.

If we want to lead (guide, influence, direct, inspire change in) people, we can do so through engaging and challenging their narratives. Where are they on their search for a hero? What struggles and conflicts do they see themselves facing? Can you be the aid or mentor who cares enough to enter their narratives with encouragement and support? Can you challenge their current narratives to help them see Christ as the only hero who can provide freedom?

Jesus often entered people's narratives through the use of stories and parables because it was the most direct way to communicate enormous truths. This type of leadership requires no further degrees, certifications, trainings, or titles. That's a relief. Life has already equipped you with all the material you need. You don't need to (and shouldn't) memorize any of my stories; they won't be as powerful as your own. You don't need to be creative or clever to be a storied leader. All you need is an authentic relationship with Christ, a desire to want that for others, and a willingness to share your story well.

Reflect or Discuss

1. When you reflect on the story of your life, in what ways does it reflect the classic narrative pattern (setting, rising action, conflicts, falling action, resolution)?

2. How did your own conversion experience to some extent reflect the Monomyth pattern of seeking resolution for problems too big for you to solve? How does your continued growth in Christ still reflect this?

3. In what ways can you relate to the human tendency to cast relationships, things, addictions, or ourselves as the heroes in our lives?

4. How have you personally observed the futility of making these things heroes in your life, or perhaps in the life of someone else?

5. How can you function as an aid, mentor, or friend to speak into another's faith narrative journey?

SECTION TWO

KNOWING MY STORY AND YOURS

Before the age of DVDs, movie rental, video streaming, hundreds of channels, and on-demand media services, life was different. If we wanted to watch a particular television show, we had to watch it on the precise day and at the precise time that it aired. If not, we lost out. If we missed *Miracle on 34th Street*, we'd have to wait another 364 days before our next opportunity. It was a miracle, indeed, that any of us survived these media droughts of yesteryear.

One such show that my family waited all year to view was *The Wizard of Oz*. Although a heartwarming classic, it evoked just enough fear to keep us seated closely on the couch. Those flying monkeys still haunt me! I was always relieved, however, when the Wicked Witch finally melted. Good had prevailed over evil, reinforcing the fairly simple narrative I held for life, until 2003.

In 2003, the Curran Theatre in San Francisco held the premiere of what would become one of the most popular musicals ever: *Wicked*. Based on the 1995 novel by Gregory Maguire, this musical challenged what had once been my simple narrative.

Although she is thoroughly wicked by the time Dorothy meets her, Maguire's version of her history invites the audience to consider that perhaps Elphaba (the Wicked Witch of the West) hasn't always been that way. As their backstories are examined, we discover that Elphaba's relationship with Glinda (the Good Witch) is more complicated than what appears on the surface in Dorothy's story. We develop empathy for her. Along with leaving the theater humming very catchy songs, we might also leave with a greater appreciation for the practice and necessity of listening to one's backstory. Individual narratives are often more complex than appearances may indicate.

Effective communication always hinges upon understanding. In order to connect with another human being, I first need to know who I am. In other words, what's *my* story? How has the good news of the gospel affected my life? Second, I need to know who the other is. In other words, what's *his* or *her* story? This happens through effective listening. Although it sounds easy, listening is hard work. But if I care enough to listen, I hold the potential to truly understand another. If you know your story and listen to mine, you can connect with me.

4 The Art of the Before-and-After Story

*...Always be prepared to give an answer to
everyone who asks you to give the reason
for the hope that you have...*
—1 Peter 3:15

Storied leadership involves the intentional use of story and narrative to influence and lead others. Sometimes this means speaking to a large group. Sometimes it means engaging on social media. Other times it means expressing an idea to a church board. And, most often, it means a one-on-one conversation. Regardless of the context and medium, however, storied leadership begins by knowing my story of Christ's transformation in my own life. But how much detail should I provide? There's so much I could and want to share, so what do I include, and what do I leave out?

Pastor and author Bill Hybels, in *Just Walk Across the Room*,[1] implies that there are at least four really bad ways to tell our story to others.

1. **Long-windedness**. It's tempting to tell too much, too soon. This wears the listener out. Hybels suggests the importance of monitoring the listener's nonverbal behavior. Is she fidgeting, shifting her weight a lot, or nervously looking around? The story of what Christ has done for you is fascinating, but tell it

briefly, knowing that listeners can always ask follow-up questions to signal that they want more.

2. **Fuzziness**. Your faith story needs clarity. If you ask for my faith story, I could tell you about my first encounters with faith in Green Bay. I could then explain how my family moved to a farm, where we attended a small country church and how my faith developed in the small youth group. I could tell you about late-night faith conversations with my third-floor Hills Hall buddies at Olivet Nazarene University. Then I could share some victories I won around an altar as a newlywed living in southern Illinois. But all that would just be confusing. Hybels urges us instead to avoid multiple plot lines in the initial telling of our story to someone. If the listener is investing all his mental energy in simply trying to follow my story, he is probably missing the most important part—*that Christ changed my life.*

3. *Religionese*. We've all heard testimonies filled with abstract religious language. It's really a matter of audience analysis. Among other believers who share our faith lexicon, expressions like *becoming fully sanctified, dying to self,* or *filled with the Holy Ghost* have deep meaning and are understood by the listener. To one who does not believe, these phrases may hold no meaning at all. Worse, they could trigger connotations that confuse, if not frighten, them. *Who wants to die? Do I really want a ghost living in me? Is sanctification some New-Age, out-of-body, mystical experience?*

4. **Superiority**. I rejoice in the knowledge that I am a child of the King. I have the risen Savior living in me. Through Christ's sacrifice, I am saved from the bondage of sin. Living in but not of this world, I am set apart. These are all pretty amazing things, right? I could go on and on about how the Lord works in and through me, and all of it would be true. Yet, if I'm not careful, I can give off an air of superiority and arrogance to an unbeliever. *You're the one who's messed up without Christ; I'm the one with all the answers. I live a perfect life free of mistakes, temptations, and bad decisions.* This is not exactly an attractive—or accu-

rate—message to send, even if it's unintentional. My story *must* reflect humility.

□　□　□

You visit your aunt Matilda's cabin in the woods of northern Wisconsin. Your surroundings are beautiful, but it's a cyber wasteland. You know those maps showing off a mobile phone company's coverage? Look closely; the area you're in now isn't colored in.

You arrive in time to have brats off the grill, apple pie, and good conversation. But now Aunt Matilda is off to bed because it's so late. Not sure what to do with yourself at…eight thirty p.m., you reach for your smartphone. No service. You walk around the starlit yard, holding the phone heavenward, hoping for a flickering, moonlit bar of hope. Nothing.

You head back in and look for the remote to the 1970s-model television. No remote. Is that sweat forming on your forehead? Rediscovering the concept of knobs and dials on a television, you fumble around until a blue dot grows into a glowing picture. You beam with joy as if having discovered electricity itself. Adjusting the rabbit ears, you realize there is no HD. No On-Demand. No Netflix. There are, in fact, exactly three channels. One is mostly static and fuzz with the occasional scrolling white lines. The other is a community cable-access show featuring a panel discussion on lakeshore erosion. So far, lakeshore erosion is in the lead.

The third channel comes in fairly clearly, even in color. It's a physically fit man in workout clothes standing near what appears to either be a medieval torture device or some kind of exercise equipment. It's an infomercial! He looks intensely at the camera as he enthusiastically reads off the teleprompter. Text scrolls across the screen in white, capitalized, bold font:

- **YOU MUST EXERCISE 30 MINUTES, AT LEAST 3 TIMES A WEEK TO MAINTAIN YOUR CARDIORESPIRATORY ENDURANCE**
- **YOU NEED TO INCREASE YOUR AEROBIC THRESHOLD TO AN ELEVATION BETWEEN 20 AND 35% ABOVE NORMAL**
- **YOUR RESTING METABOLIC RATE SHOULD BE LOWER THAN YOUR BASAL METABOLIC RATE**

- **YOU MUST STRIVE FOR A HEALTHY BMI**
- **EFFECTIVE EXERCISE INVOLVES CLOSE MONITORING OF YOUR VO2MAX**
- **YOU NEED A LIFTING ROUTINE DESIGNED WITH CAREFUL ATTENTION TO ISOTONIC WEIGHT PLACEMENT**
- **YOUR BODY NEEDS EXERCISE INTENSE ENOUGH THAT YOUR ANAEROBIC THRESHOLD LEADS TO THE ACCUMULATION OF LACTIC ACID IN THE MUSCLES**

There's more. A lot more claims. A lot more scrolling text. A lot more talking. Although the lakeshore erosion and static options are beginning to sound better, you don't feel like leaving your chair to turn the dial manually. You watch all thirty minutes, including the detailed instructions of how to send in fifteen payments of only $19.95 to receive the equipment plus a set of steak knives. Yet somehow you resist. You reach for neither your credit card nor your phone. Good thing, because your phone has no service.

For the sake of this example, let's assume you have put away a few too many brats and pies in your time and, frankly, could stand to lose a few pounds. Although this pleasantly speaking man on the television made multiple claims, promises, and a limited-time-only offer, you are still not convinced. Why? The person, the points, and the proof.

The person. The man on the screen is pleasant. He is clearly physically fit. He seems to know his facts, or at least is a good reader. But you don't know him personally. More importantly, you don't trust him. How rich will he get off of your fifteen "simple" payments? He doesn't know you. You suspect his motives are self-serving. You wish you didn't have to be this cynical, but you are.

The points. Many points were made. Unless you have prior experience with exercise science, you probably didn't understand most of the claims. There were so many, and all of them were generalized and abstract. The claims are probably true, but they don't connect with what you know. Even though they weren't scrolling all that fast, they still felt like a blur to you.

The proof. Did this man actually get in shape from using the equipment, or was he simply hired to represent it because he was already in good shape? How do I know it worked for him? More importantly, how do I know it will work for me?

Now, since you have to refill your coffee anyway, you get up and turn the knob, suddenly curious about the effects of lakeshore erosion. However, that show has ended, and what's playing now on that channel is, you guessed it, *another infomercial!* It, too, is for exercise equipment, but it has a different approach.

Instead of thirty minutes featuring some guy and scrolling, abstract claims, it features thirty-second testimonials of people claiming to have used this equipment. While we hear each speaker's voice in turn, the screen shows us their individual before-and-after photos. Wow! The message is clear: Unless these photos have been altered, these people experienced radical transformations.

The infomercial ends like the previous one. You're given details of the equipment and are encouraged to call now, while the number on the screen is blinking. *Operators are waiting to take your call!* Do you toss your cell phone and look for Aunt Matilda's landline to seal this deal? Probably not, but let's analyze it.

The person(s). Although there are a few different speakers this time, we still don't know any of them personally. We don't know their motives. Are they just paid actors? We can't exactly say we trust them.

The points. No scrolling text of abstract claims. No confusing exercise terminology. Just ordinary-looking people telling their weight-loss stories. Each of their before photos and stories was shared. One had trouble losing weight after having a baby. Another claimed he had tried multiple unsuccessful diets. Then they purchased and used the advertised equipment. Their stories shifted to their after selves. The new mother lost eighteen pounds and now feels confident going to the beach again. Another discovered he still had six-pack abs that for years had been concealed by flab.

The proof. The points and proof in this second infomercial are nearly identical. The points of what the equipment can achieve are proven by these people's before-and-after stories. They don't have to invoke authority of scientists or fitness trainers; their lives are living proof.

For a variety of reasons (still have that nagging trust issue), we may not act. But clearly this second infomercial has gotten our attention and engaged our minds with an internal conversation we can't avoid: *I can relate to the before photo; I'd like to experience the kind of change seen in the after photo.*

How often do we approach evangelism with a method similar to the first infomercial? Whether speaking to a congregation, writing a blog, or talking one on one with a friend, neighbor, coworker, or family member, we sometimes do this. Okay, probably—hopefully!—not with bold, capitalized font, but we still sometimes do this.

The person. Depending on the audience, we may not have established trust with them. They may be suspicious of our motives. *Is she just trying to win a church contest of who can bring the most people this Sunday?* (Hopefully no churches are holding contests like these for members over the age of twelve.)

The points. Using Hybels's terminology, we may be speaking in religionese, imparting great theological truths that, as of yet, hold no connection for the audience. *You want me to die to myself, be born again, and be filled with the Holy Spirit? What?* Even if they are true, our claims may be so abstract, diverse, and numerous that it becomes difficult for listeners to digest and understand. They may be listening, but what we are saying might be scrolling past them.

The proof. We are speaking from our after selves. We have already experienced a transformation in Christ, but we are speaking from the after side of transformation. It's easy for a physically fit person to tell me to lose weight; that person has no problem with weight! And it's easy for you to tell me I can turn my life around when your life appears perfect. You are an after person. But I'm still a before person.

□   □   □

Even if you are reading this book at your aunt Matilda's cabin, you don't need cell service to do what I'm about to ask of you. Get your phone and a take a selfie. If you don't have a phone or it doesn't take photos, you can do two things: 1) Consider an upgrade. 2) Hold your hand out in front of you and pretend to take a picture of yourself. It'll accomplish the same thing if you have a good imagination.

Now look at your selfie. It's who you are right now. More specifically, it's your *after* self. This is you *after* Christ has changed your life. This is the self others see. And it's not a bad thing. They see your personality, your smile, your quirks, and your sense of compassion. *But it's your after self.* You painfully know that you are not perfect and that you are still growing in Christ, but your after self doesn't necessarily reveal that to the world. Therefore, you can be intimidating. You are the perfectly fit man or woman pointing out that I'm flabby. And, for some people, that might be plenty motivating. But for a lot of us, it isn't.

Imagine with me if social media and cell phones had existed in biblical times. What if biblical characters had used social media to tell their transformation stories? Indulge me while I imagine some before-and-after biblical selfies.

Character	Before Selfie	After Selfie
Moses	Looking fearfully toward camera #MurdererInHiding	Looking confident; Red Sea visible over his shoulder #RideTheWave
David	Standing in a pasture #SheepStink	With a fallen Philistine giant in the background #SlingshotPower
Woman Caught in Adultery	Kneeling, face to the ground; angry mob stands around her #CondemnedToDie	Standing next to Jesus; no one else around #Forgiven
Thomas	Pointing toward Jesus and disciples #IDoubtIt	Touching Jesus's scars #NoDoubt
Mary	With Jesus on cross behind her #HeHasFallen	An empty tomb behind her #HeHasRisenIndeed

Get the point? The Bible is full of before-and-after stories. Thomas's faith means so much more to us when we see his doubt. Paul's zeal for the gospel means so much more when we see his former, zealous persecution of the believers. We need more than these Bible characters' after stories. We need their before *and* after stories.

Remember the notion of the universal Monomyth, described by Joseph Campbell? Nearly universally, from the first recorded stories until now, the stories that connect best with our human experience are stories about journeys—specifically, journeys in which the protagonists step out of their status quo to seek something more. Along the journey, they encounter some form of aid (a weapon, a discovered ability or strength, or more often the direct support of a friend or mentor who speaks truth into their lives). With this support, they are poised to experience supernatural transformations that leave them changed and whole.

These stories connect with us because we also see our lives as journeys on which we are seeking wholeness, peace, resolution, and freedom from whatever imprisons us. Before-and-after stories connect with us powerfully because they are mini journey stories. They reveal where you were in a conflicted part of your journey, how you found resolution, and the only hero who could possibly have gotten you through it: *Christ.*

We all see ourselves going through life as a journey. These journeys will present many conflicts, barriers, and snares. In those moments, our hero's journey begins. Although we may initially cast ourselves as hero, we learn—possibly the hard way—that we cannot save ourselves. If I'm stuck in my before, seeking an after, and you connect with me using your before-and-after story, your story inspires me to seek the same hero who saved and changed you.

While we could tell it in a long version, we could also express it in less than a minute. The second infomercial didn't show pictures from each day of the sixty-day exercise regime, just two—the before and the after. It includes no long-winded explanations, fuzziness, religionese, or superiority. Interested viewers of the infomercial can call or go online if they want more details. If listeners want us to share more details of our before-and-after faith stories, we should be more than willing.

Before and After Jesus

When we think about our before-and-after stories, we tend to think of one big story—how we found Christ. That is our best story because it is what changed our journey most radically. For some, this story is vivid, and marked by major life changes. *My gambling addiction cost me my family and led me to theft. After I surrendered my life to the Lord, he helped me leave my life of crime and slowly earn back the trust of my wife and children.*

Some of us, by wonderful grace, came to a relationship with God before we could tie our own shoes. Typically these before-and-after stories are not marked with dramatic life changes like freedom from gambling and theft—unless, of course, you were one *really* bad kid. My second-grade teacher once publicly accused me of cutting the tail off our class gerbil with a razor blade. For the record, I didn't do it. Sometimes I wish I had, just so my own childhood salvation story might sound, well, more exciting.

Yet my story, and any story of salvation, *is* exciting. God intervened in my life as a young boy, saving me from the risk of ever entering into a gambling addiction and life of crime (or other life entrapments). To me, that seems perhaps even more powerful a story than having to suffer the pain and consequences. Whatever your salvation story is, it is exciting—not because of what you did or didn't do before or after it took place. *It's exciting because of what Christ did.*

But what about your before-and-after story from today? What has the Lord done in your life today? What would you be like this afternoon had God not worked in your life this morning? Christ tells us in Luke 9:23 that if we are to be his disciples, we are to pick up our crosses daily and follow him. What struggles, doubts, fears, or temptations did you have to surrender to Christ today? These daily moments of growth in Christ constitute volumes of before-and-after stories that we accumulate and have at our fingertips to share. Your friend is struggling with the issue of faith. How can she believe something she cannot see? What is your most recent before-and-after story where God taught or retaught you about faith? What hope do you hold today where, just yesterday, you were gripped by fear?

You do not merely have one before-and-after selfie. What journeys have you been on *recently* where Christ has changed you? Which one does someone in your life need to hear today? If you can't think of anything, that's a problem because we both know only Christ is perfect. So if you have no recent before-and-after faith stories to share, you need to stop reading this book and return to God's book. There are undoubtedly wonderful ways God wants to enter your journey today, leaving you changed into a new after. And what a great story that'll be!

Perhaps your church has held a service featuring cardboard testimonies. If not, you might see what you can do about making it happen because they are powerful! Interested members are given a large piece of flat cardboard and a thick, black marker. On one side of the board, they write one sentence, phrase, or even a single word that describes something from their before story. *Imprisoned by fear and self-doubt.* On the other side, they write a similarly worded after message that reflects how Christ has changed them. *Set free! Confident in Christ!* Other examples include:

- Not able to make ends meet / God provided!
- Was a passive, sideline Christian / Now living my faith out loud!
- Divorced, angry, hurt, broken / Found wholeness in Christ!
- Was unhappy and unsatisfied / Jesus filled me with joy!
- Losing my hearing / Learning to hear God's voice!
- Was an orphan at age 2 / God found me parents!
- Parents broke up / God kept me together!
- Lost my son / God gave me lots of harvest field kids!
- Lied to my parents / God taught me the truth!
- Doctor said it was cancer / God performed a miracle!

As they take turns walking across the platform, they stop in the middle and hold up the before side for all to see. Then they flip the board around for all to see the after. No words are spoken. The simply worded before-and-after message tells the entire story, and the only hero is Christ because he is the one who changed the before into the after. Some churches make videos to illustrate these stories instead of doing it live, but either way, the experience is electrifying. The simple before-and-after story sends one message: *Christ changed my life, and he can change yours too.*

What is *your* before-and-after story?

Reflect or Discuss

1. Which of the ineffective ways of telling a story have you been guilty of doing when trying to share your faith story? What effect(s) might it have had on your listener(s)?

2. How would you tell someone your before-and-after selfie—your sixty-second testimony of how Christ changed your life?

3. Think back over the past few weeks. What are some before-and-after testimonies that you have for what the Lord has done in your life recently? Whom do you know who might be encouraged to hear these?

4. When sharing your own personal before-and-after faith story with another, how is it likely to be effective based on the *person,* the *points,* and the *proof*?

5. If you were to display a cardboard testimony today, what would the front (before) and the back (after) say?

5 Listening to the Backstory

Which of you, if his son asks for bread,
will give him a stone?
—Matthew 7:9

The Second Bottle

In my Christmas stocking I found three individually wrapped, sample-sized bottles of cologne—each a different brand, each containing an ounce of slightly different hues of blue fluid. *That's nice,* I thought. *I don't want to stink.* They were tiny bottles, though, so I knew they wouldn't last very long. After shaving the next morning, I reached for one of them, sprayed it, and felt the cool burn. Smelled nice.

The next day, I reached for the second, slightly different-shaped bottle. That one smelled great. Although I can literally go several years without another human complimenting my scent, that day I had two students *and* my daughter tell me I smelled good. Did this indicate I normally smelled horrible? Something to ponder.

I never even reached for the third bottle. Day after day I kept using the second bottle. I liked the smell and suddenly had that teeny-tiny, extra sense of confidence leaving the house with it on. (Does this make me sound insecure?)

My birthday came about a month after Christmas. My wife, Jeanette, handed me a wrapped box. In it was a significantly *larger*-sized bottle of—you guessed it—the cologne from bottle number two! I looked astonished because I had never told her my preference, but she explained. "I checked the cabinet to see which bottle was nearly empty so I could tell which one was your favorite." I was pleased, and I think she was even more pleased because she had given me a gift she knew *I* wanted—not just a gift she wanted *for* me.

Garrison Keillor, of *Prairie Home Companion* fame, wrote a poignant essay on this subject for the Lands' End catalog in 1997 titled "What I'm Giving You for Christmas."[1] Keillor observes that when we give gifts, we are essentially acting on a theory of who we think the receiver is, or *should* be.

Jeanette comes from a bowling family. Her mother, father, and brother were all good bowlers and active in local bowling leagues. She, therefore, could have given me a bowling ball or bowling shoes for my birthday. She could have even given me a membership to our local bowling alley or signed me up with a league. After all, bowling is a fun hobby and can be a great family activity or a social opportunity with friends. For the members of her family, these would have been highly thoughtful gifts. But I don't bowl. A few times a year I enjoy trying to break a score of 100 in a game with my family, but that's plenty for me. I can respect and appreciate the ability of good bowlers who make it look easy, but it's not easy for me. So Jeanette giving me a bowling-related gift in hopes of getting me interested in bowling would not have lit up my eyes as much as fulfilling the desire I currently had for cologne. I would have politely thanked her (I hope!), but the ball would have collected dust for an appropriate number of years before appearing in a rummage sale with a green sticker reading, *$1.00, never used.*

Giving Bread

Storied leadership is not merely about the telling of stories. It may not always involve *telling* a story at all. The more important precursor to telling stories is *listening* to stories. How can a leader suggest where one should go without knowing where that person currently is? Additionally, it may be equally difficult to understand where someone is (story) before discerning where that person has been (backstory). Once we understand one's story and backstory, we are in a position to form a compassionate response—whether that involves the specific telling of a story or not. Whichever seems to be the most appropriate response, we are engaging a person's narrative.

When explaining in Matthew 7:7–8 how those who ask will receive, Jesus offers some perspective with a quick analogy of father and son. "Which of you, if your son asks for bread, will give him a stone? Or if he asks for a fish, will give him a snake?" A loving parent listens to what a child wants and needs, and desires to give it to the child.

Fred Craddock reminds us: "Communication is difficult. How do you bridge that distance? It is a great distance between those who hear and those of us who speak. We think all of this is clear. It has been rolled out neatly and in order, but one thing we usually forget is the location of the person who's listening."[2]

As storied leaders, we listen to learn where people are in their faith narratives right now. What conflicts have arisen in their journeys for which they need resolution? Without effectively listening, we are essentially operating based on our predetermined theories of who these people are. Without knowing individuals' stories and backstories, we are forced to fill in the gaps with our assumptions, prejudices, and biases. Our communication, then, becomes the giving of stones and snakes.

If evangelism involves encouraging one to a closer relationship with Christ, I need to know that person's story. But, assuming I haven't known this person my entire life, my perspective is limited to a fairly one-dimensional image. I see what you look like *now*. I have observed (or heard from you) what you are going through *now*. I care about your decisions *now*. I also care about your *future* and want to speak encouragement into your narrative to inspire you toward change. By focusing only on the *now* and the *future*, however, my ability as a storied leader may be limited.

I don't have to be a licensed therapist to care about where you've been. A person's present disbelief is predicated on some past experience. Each of us has a backstory—a narrative of where we've been, what we've done, what we've heard, and what we've seen. And our unique composite of these experiences paints our faith picture. For some, the composite portrays an angry, vindictive God; for others, a God who is indifferent to loss and suffering; and for still others, the faith picture involves hypocrisy, legalism, or judgmental condemnation.

I could share my before-and-after story about how the Lord intervened in our adoption process by miraculously providing the necessary financial resources. But it might not be the right story for the person who recently experienced a failed adoption attempt. The story is true, but it may be received like a stone. As trivial as a bottle of cologne seems, the giving of it on my birthday represented Jeanette's careful observation of my needs and preferences, which put her in a position to offer an appropriate gift based on who I am as a person. In essence, she gave me bread rather than a stone.

Listening for Leakage

If effective storied leadership hinges on choosing stories most likely to inspire change in someone, I must first listen. I must listen to what people say as well as what they don't say. I must also be attentive to body language and nonverbal responses. For example, do they tend to bristle with discomfort when talking about a particular, faith-related topic? Do they project a sense of defensiveness when saying they used to attend church but now are just too busy?

In the late 1960s, Paul Ekman and Wallace Friesen coined the phrase "nonverbal leakage"[3] to describe the often involuntary display of nonverbal messages through our body language. For example, a child lying to his parent may not even be aware that he is wringing his hands and that his cheeks are flushed. A boss may be confronting my behavior, yet I notice his hands slightly shaking and a rapid breathing rate. Beyond his verbal message about my behavior, it is very clear to me that this situation makes him highly uncomfortable.

Although experienced liars have worked to control or mask such displays, the rest of us often give off nonverbal cues that betray how we feel. Since conservative estimates suggest that nearly 75 percent of communicative meaning comes nonverbally, we need to be listening to more than a person's words. When a person's words don't seem to match the body language, we tend to believe the body language over the words. It's easy to control a verbal message (e.g., "I'm fine"), but it's difficult to control our nonverbal messages (e.g., a voice that quivers as it says, "I'm fine"). The nonverbal leakage gives us away.

The challenge, then, is to listen beyond the mere words being spoken. After Christmas, I could have told Jeanette that I liked the three sample-sized colognes equally. But my behavior—nearly draining one bottle while avoiding the others—sent a different message. If my words had conflicted with my behavior, she would have believed my behavior.

Effective communication requires an accurate understanding of the other person. If you know me and my backstory, you can adapt your message appropriately. If I openly tell you where I am in my faith journey, then you know where to begin. If I don't, you need to keep listening to my words, but you also need to listen to what I reveal nonverbally through my body language, behavior, and choices. In their study of nonverbal communication, Ekman and Friesen describe how our bodies unconsciously reveal messages through *adapters, regulators,* and nonverbal *congruence.*[4]

Adapters. Even if our words express confidence, our bodies often find ways of releasing inner tension through the use of nonverbal adapters. Each of us is different in this regard. My hands may begin to tremble. You may twist your necklace, nervously play with your hair, or rub your fingers together. There are countless ways our bodies betray our confidence by giving away our inner state of discomfort, nervousness, or anxiety. If the person I'm listening to demonstrates adapters at particular parts of our conversation, that may indicate that a backstory has been triggered.

Of course, not every nervous gesture contains meaning or is something into which we should read too much. Everyone has a baseline, or norm, of behavior. Only when we know another person fairly well can we distinguish the presence of some adaptive behavior distinct from that person's normal behavior.

When talking about forgiveness, does she begin to shuffle her feet, touch her face, or twist her necklace—when she normally does not do these things? Or does he fold his arms in front of him, look around the room, or even seem to squint just a bit when you suggest that his children might enjoy your Sunday school programs? He may verbally thank you for the invitation, but his adapters may indicate a triggered backstory that is making him uncomfortable. It may not be the right time or place to probe into the backstories that may be triggering this tension, but it's important to recognize (and remember) the triggers.

Regulators. Our need to control is great, and we do it in conversations in many ways, including nonverbally. We may raise a finger slightly to indicate a desire to interject. A hand could be asking the speaker to pause or stop. A slightly opened mouth and/or raised eyebrows may indicate our intention to speak a sudden thought. Shutting our eyes while speaking may send the message we don't want to be interrupted. After all, if I can't see your nonverbal cues indicating you want to interject, I can hold the floor and keep talking without seeming rude. Pretty clever, huh?

We use body language intentionally and unconsciously to indicate a desire to speak. But our body language may also reflect our desire to switch topics or end the conversation. A person's use of adapters may function in this way. Similarly, looking at one's watch, taking a couple steps backward, putting on a coat, or shuffling things in one's hands may all signal one's desire to wrap this up.

Changes in our tone of voice and breathing send the same messages, often in conjunction with other nonverbal messages. She looks at her watch while taking a deep, audible breath. He shuffles his feet while saying, "Wellll...alllllright then." Regulating conversation is a necessary, untaught skill most of us have, but are regulators simply being used to indicate appropriate closure at the end of a discussion? Or might someone be using them mid-conversation to indicate discomfort with a particular topic? Again, this may not be the time to push or ask about the discomfort, but as storied leaders, we want to be sensitive to topics that may trigger backstory blocks.

Congruence. I was at a social event recently with my preteen daughter, Lucy. I was very uncomfortable with how the event was unfolding, although I thought I was masking it well. At one point Lucy looked up at me and asked, "Dad, how are you doing?"

"I'm doing fine," I lied, smiling.

Without hesitation, she followed with, "Are you the *real* kind of fine?"

She knew my baseline behavior well enough to know I was not fine. She knew there was some backstory explaining why this event was bothering me.

When our words don't match our actions and behavior, we lack congruence. To total strangers, this might be missed because they don't know our baseline. In a friendship, however, the incongruence is often obvious, which explains why we can often tell whether someone will actually show up at an event after verbally expressing an intent to do so. The verbal may have been a yes, but the nonverbal suggested otherwise. Congruence also affirms the growing focus on evangelism being a relational process. The better we come to know others, the better we become at reading their nonverbal behaviors.

Listening may imply a focus on words alone. Effective listening, however, is so much broader. It involves observing and perceiving how things are said and the myriad of body language that accompanies it. When words and body language aren't congruent, we are usually safe believing the body. Words are easy to control; body language is not. Therefore, it tends to be a more accurate barometer for how a person is truly feeling in a conversation. Going deeper with a topic (or continuing the conversation at all) might be like handing a snake or stone to one whose body language suggests a backstory of discomfort.

☐ ☐ ☐

When she was only six years old, our oldest daughter, Rachel, looked up at me as I tucked her in to bed and said, "I hate this bed."

She was referring to her waterbed, which I had made for her, complete with custom drawers. Yes, I was proud of my craftsmanship, so this declaration struck a nerve. I asked why. She mumbled a few goofy reasons about it not being soft enough, hard enough, warm enough, long enough, short enough—you get the picture. The response in my mind was something like this: *You ungrateful little child!* Fortunately, an unusual (for me) spirit of discernment held my tongue.

When she had run out of things she disliked about it, I simply said, "Rachel, what's bothering you?"

Long silence. Tears. Then the backstory came out. Before moving to this new town, she and I had developed a Saturday morning routine of taking the city bus to a doughnut shop. It was our special time as dad and daughter. That routine had not been replaced after the move. Without the ability to express her hurt directly, Rachel directed her anger toward something she knew I valued. It got my attention.

For a variety of reasons, many people are like this when it comes to discussions about faith. Instead of expressing real issues of hurt, doubt, or fear, the nonbelievers we encounter might instead provide a variety of masks: excuses, justifications, attacks against organized religion, and even personal attacks on ourselves, our church, or our pastor. Effective listening can help us determine what the real issues are. Specifically:

- Does the sheer number and variety of disconnected responses suggest the presence of a primary central issue not being verbalized? Sometimes the presence of many minor reasons hides the absence of the single major one.

- Are there a lot of adapters? Is the person saying he's fine but a change in typical body language sends an opposite message?

- Is there a lack of congruence? Is the other person claiming one thing but her choices contradict it?

- Is an individual or group offering evasive responses (e.g., *that's interesting, makes sense, sounds like a good idea, perhaps,* etc.), instead of affirmative or clear responses (*I agree, I can't support that, we should move ahead on this,* etc.)?

Had I started responding to each of Rachel's criticisms of her bed, I might never have discovered the real issue. With her, simply asking, "What's bothering you?" triggered her disclosure of the real issue. True, she was only six. But asking open-ended questions followed by a willingness to wait for responses can be just as effective with adults. When I believe I know what a person is thinking or feeling, I'm more tempted to interrupt before they finish, or offer a response even before they start to explain.

Effective listening requires me to ask open-ended questions and *wait*. Leading questions can create defensiveness because they imply judgment or an intention of the receiver. Closed questions can usually be answered with just one-word responses, like yes or no. For example:

Why don't you like our church anymore? (This is a leading question that immediately puts the other on the defensive.)

We've missed you at church. (This is an open statement that invites response, doesn't insert judgment, and creates the space for as much or as little response as the listener is comfortable sharing at this point.)

Do you agree with the proposed changes for worship services? (This is a closed question that does not invite the person to offer more than a potentially ambiguous, simple response.)

What are your thoughts on the proposed changes for worship services? (This is an open-ended question that allows the person to provide reasoning in addition to a simple statement in favor or against.)

Paraphrasing and Perception-Checking

Strong listeners first seek to understand before being understood. But how do we know if we understand? Maybe the sudden shuffling of feet and looking around the room indicate one's realization of a missed appointment rather than discomfort with the conversation. The problem with body language (and much of communication in general) is that it can be highly ambiguous. It's easy to misinterpret and receive messages that were never intended. Similarly, it's easy to miss the intended ones.

The best way to check the effectiveness of our listening is through paraphrasing. After a board member expresses her concerns about a motion to purchase new carpeting, I could offer this paraphrase: "Joan, let me make sure I understand you. Because the bids for new carpeting are coming in so high, you think we should hold off for now? Is that accurate?"

At this point, Joan can verify my understanding with a simple yes. Or she can correct my understanding: "No, that's not what I'm saying at all. I think we need to purchase the carpet now. I'm just concerned about the high bids and think we should at least go back and see if these are their best numbers."

The paraphrase reveals my level of understanding, and the final question, "Is that correct?" allows the other person to verify that my understanding was accurate, or to correct what I misinterpreted.

To examine another example, put yourself in this scenario. After asking an unbeliever about his faith journey, he discloses that his upbringing occurred in a very legalistic religious environment. He offers three different examples of innocent-sounding things he and his siblings were not allowed to do because they were banned by his church. As the conversation continues, he also shares that, since he now works six days a week, it is difficult to get out of bed on Sunday morning for church.

After listening, you offer a paraphrase and perception check. "I understand how getting out on your only day off doesn't sound fun, but it sounds like what's really keeping you away is a pretty legalistic background that seemed to really confuse, if not hurt, you. Is that accurate?"

Paraphrasing and checking our perceptions helps confirm or deny the accuracy of our listening. Equally important is that practicing these elements of effective listening demonstrates our desire to understand. If we truly care, we listen in order to understand. And when people sense that we understand, they know we care.

Reflect or Discuss

1. In what ways can you relate to Garrison Keillor's notion of having theories of other people that are often based on our own wants, needs, and understandings?

2. How do our assumptions of others limit our desire to actively listen to them? What is often the result?

3. How can you increase your attention to and awareness of others' body language to read their unspoken messages?

4. To minimize misunderstanding, how can you utilize paraphrasing and perception-checking to verify what you've heard or observed (nonverbally) in another person?

6 Detecting Dissonance

I must listen to people's backstories so I can effectively connect with them—give them bread, not stones. I must listen not only to the verbal but also to the nonverbal. I either know (from things she's disclosed to me) or suspect (from some nonverbal incongruence) the presence of backstory blocks in her faith story. But once I have an idea of some of her faith blocks, what do I do with them? Effective listening helps me detect dissonance. And while I can't change a person's backstory, my storied leadership can inspire her to allow Christ to transform it.

The brain craves a sense of balance, an internal consistency. We need our beliefs to harmonize with each other. For instance, I have various beliefs about my wife. I believe she cares about me and will not intentionally hurt me. I also believe she is honest with me and wouldn't intentionally hide information from me that I would want or need to know. To psychologist Leon Festinger, this means my mind can enjoy a state of cognitive consonance, or balance of beliefs.[1]

But what if you told me that Jeanette has been secretly replacing my cholesterol medication with sugar pills over the past several months? To Festinger, this would mean my brain would lose its consonance—finding itself in *cognitive dissonance*. My former balance and mental equilibrium would be threatened by this new information. How can she love me, be honest with me, and want the best for me while at the same time attempting to harm me? This new claim, if true, doesn't fit my former belief system. The brain cannot exist in this state of imbalance. It must restore consonance.

Cognitive Dissonance theory suggests that when our brains face this kind of sudden internal dissonance, they will restore the balance through one or more of these options:

1. **Ignore**. We can avoid, distort, or discount the dissonant message. Using my example, I could refuse to listen to your accusation, or simply assume you are wrong or crazy. No more dissonance, and no change to my beliefs.

2. **Add information**. We can seek consonant information to support our threatened belief. For instance, I could acknowledge your claim as true but seek evidence that my cholesterol medication was actually unnecessary. No more dissonance. No change in my belief about Jeanette being kind.

3. **Change**. We can change our former belief or attitude. I could realize your new claim is correct and realize that my wife is actually trying to harm me. No more dissonance. Now I have a new and stable belief: My wife is out to get me. I have restored consonance through a personal transformation. I have *changed* my thinking.

Dealing with Dissonance

The apostle Paul reminds us that "the message of the cross is foolishness to those who are perishing, but to us who are being saved it is the power of God" (1 Corinthians 1:18). Hearing the gospel creates dissonance in the mind of the unbeliever—or at least it should. Giving my life to Christ represents a radical change from living life for myself. Seeking fulfillment, peace, and salvation through Christ is a huge change from my former search in places that only brought emptiness.

It's no surprise that any form of evangelism would bring discomfort and a state of dissonance to a hearer. And if Festinger was right, one could choose to ignore the gospel message. He could even distort or discount it as untrue or invalid. He could also seek additional information or evidence to support his disbelief. Any of these responses would help restore his cognitive consonance. He has found justification to resist the gospel message. It is no longer threatening to him.

Yet he could also reduce the sudden dissonance by recognizing the truth of the gospel. He can find a new state of internal balance and peace by accepting the new message, and Christ, into his life. In oit he could allow the truth of the gospel to *change* him.

The reason the gospel creates such dissonance in unbelievers is that it doesn't fit their current belief structures. Those structures are the result of a lifetime of experiences that have created complex back-stories. They may include previous negative experiences with church or Christians. They could include observed hypocrisy, personal loss, intellectual arguments, painful judgment, rejection, or self-loathing. Therefore, the message of a loving Father, forgiveness, freedom from sin, and eternal life may cause enormous dissonance.

Storied leadership can play a role in helping nonbelievers bring consonance back to their belief structures. We know the Lord relentlessly pursues and convicts. God's conviction is the most powerful form of cognitive dissonance, pressing people toward a response (avoid and justify, or accept and change). If we are willing and available, our interactions can be used by the Lord as part of this process, but we must be careful not to become one more Christian in the list of those who have hurt them.

Stories offer us the opportunity for powerful connection and identification. You sharing your before-and-after story can therefore create dissonance for me. It may provoke an internal conversation within me in which I realize my life may be similar to the way yours was before you accepted Christ. Your life after encountering Christ may represent the kind of peace (hence, consonance) that I desire.

Your genuine and personal stories about forgiveness and grace may likewise trigger dissonance as the Lord uses them to paint an image of what my soul craves yet lacks. As storied leaders, we do not create the dissonance, but our communication can trigger an internal conversation in which a hearer perceives conviction. Storied leadership doesn't force change; it simply enters a person's narrative, challenging that person toward change. Our own changed lives are our most powerful evidence and proof. Consonance for the hearer, then, can be found in Christ.

As storied leaders, we want to use our own stories to help inspire change in others toward Christ. It's not merely our theory of who we want them to become; it's what we know they need most. My arrogance presumes to know *what* one needs the most; my confidence, however, presumes to know *whom* one needs most, and that is Christ. What loving parent would give a snake, stone, or even a bowling ball when what their child wants is bread? People need the bread of life; they may not yet want it, and their lack of desire may evoke dissonance. This is a wonderful thing for storied leaders because we know this leaves them with three options: avoiding, adding information, or changing.

Fixing the Main Break

My son-in-law works for the local water company. Subzero Illinois temperatures in winter result in many overtime hours for Andrew because of water main breaks. City water is distributed to neighborhoods through a system of underground pipes. Larger, central pipes carry water into the neighborhoods, where they branch off into smaller pipes that eventually deliver water to your faucets. The large, central—or main—pipes are buried out of view. As they age and become brittle, they are vulnerable. Prolonged freezing temperatures result in main breaks. We don't see where the main break is; we just notice low or no water pressure at our sink. We call for help.

Andrew may take our call, but he doesn't come into our home to look at our nonfunctioning faucet. He looks for the source of the break in the main. He uses high- (and some pretty low-) tech tools that allow him to listen for the sound of water rushing—indicating the source of the break. Pretty cool, huh? Once the break is found, the backhoes dig down, and the pressure is relieved until the main break can be repaired. Once it is fixed, I can finally take my shower.

Dissonance works in much the same way. The source of one's dissonance is often difficult to detect. Instead, we see its results: a family leaving the church, a man uninterested in faith, a woman with bitterness toward God. No water flowing. As storied leaders, we need to move beyond the faucet to the source of the main break, which will require listening for the backstory. Backhoes may not be warranted, but clearly it may require some digging.

When it comes to *fixing* the sources of dissonance, the water main analogy is no longer useful. Andrew, as a crew leader, has the power to fix main breaks, but we do not fix people. Similarly, we do not attempt to manipulate others into dissonance or cause conviction. This is the work of the Holy Spirit. What we can do, however, is challenge one's broken narrative with one that is whole.

Water gushing from a main pipe is a problem that cannot be avoided. Some things that lead to dissonance, however, can be. One of the hardest things we had to do as parents was break up our son's high school garage band, comprised of four very close friends of many years. Over time, they allowed some negative influences into their lives. Instead of being positive influences on each other's faith development, their friendships became toxic. They were great young men individually, but together they were walking down unhealthy paths. The band had become a source of dissonance for our son. It broke our hearts to break it up, and it broke his heart more. The band was all that mattered to his story. But that band's narrative identity created dissonance in his faith narrative.

I'm thankful to report that, in time, things improved dramatically, due in part to the mere avoidance of the source of dissonance. After identifying dissonance, we can encourage others to avoid those sources if avoidance is practical and possible. Is there a correlation between a teenager's increased dependence on social media and her lowered self-esteem? Does a friend face continual discouragement and degradation from a dating partner? Does your church board or pastor feel discouraged running under one hundred members after reading books that measure ministry success by numbers? If you can identify correlations like these, the resulting dissonance may be creating unhealthy narrative identities. As leaders, we can encourage some avoidance of these sources in each case.

Avoiding sources of dissonant information is appropriate when the information being gleaned is actually untruthful. Sometimes the information *is* truthful and cannot be avoided. Adults who were abused as children may experience dissonance with the ability to see God as loving or themselves as lovable. This backstory narrative cannot and should not be avoided. But even this dissonance can be slowly relieved with the addition of new, truthful information.

In a great book called *Difficult Conversations*, the authors refer to this as the "yes, and" approach to difficult conversations.[2] It may seem small, but the difference between "yes, and" and "yes, but" is huge. "Yes, and" recognizes the truth of both pieces of information while the "but" tends to minimize or cancel out the truth of what was stated first. We can acknowledge the unpleasant and truthful reality while recognizing that there is more to the story. Yes, bad things happen to good people, *and* God is still love. Yes, cancer has been diagnosed, *and* the Lord is still the master physician. Yes, we may be facing a mountain, *and* the Lord still moves mountains. A person's faith narrative can be incomplete due to dissonance from harsh truths. As storied leaders, we can acknowledge the truth of their narratives and add the truth of the gospel to help complete the story.

The final method of reducing dissonance is to change. The main break might not be avoided or added onto but may simply need to be replaced. So it is with our narratives. Hypochondriasis is a condition in which a person believes he is sick when in reality he is not. But he truly thinks it, and can actually experience headaches, fatigue, muscle tension, and other symptoms as a result. To the hypochondriac, being sick becomes the narrative. It isn't true, but it is reality for that person. A growing way of treating hypochondriasis is cognitive behavioral therapy, which attempts to change and replace unhelpful thinking. Although it is incredibly difficult, the hypochondriac is challenged to adopt a new narrative.

A life without bodily health is a real narrative to the hypochondriac. A life without the hope of Christ is just as real to the unbeliever. The cycle of his hero's journey consists of struggles and a search for solutions that ultimately don't satisfy. Symptoms of hopelessness and the lack of peace are real to the unbeliever, even though we know they don't have to be. As storied leaders, we can speak into others' lives to challenge their present narratives. One's source of dissonance may require more than mere avoidance or adding more information. It may require a total transformation—the acceptance of a new narrative. In short, we can use story to inspire change.

It is an exchange of narratives, the difference as drastic as before-and-after selfies. The alcoholic's narrative identity of being hopeless and dependent on the bottle can be replaced with a new story of finding hope in dependence on Christ. The change comes from Christ, not ourselves.

Consider Paul's conversion, the transformation of the woman caught in adultery, or the Roman jailer (and his whole family). Consonance, or internal peace, is finally attained when we allow the Holy Spirit to transform our story, giving us a new testimony.

Reflect or Discuss

1. In what ways can a person's backstory often reveal the source of their faith dissonance?

2. Although our temptation is often to respond or react to a person's expressed problem (like the faucet not working), discuss how the real problem (the main break) sometimes lies elsewhere.

3. The author suggests that sometimes avoiding sources of dissonance is an appropriate action. What are some examples of things, people, or media that cause unnecessary dissonance?

4. How does the "yes, and" response serve to validate one's feelings while adding additional information to his or her understanding?

5. How is the process of changing one's present identity often a process of changing the self-narrative? How can we assist in this process?

SECTION THREE

CHOOSE YOUR DESTINATION

Destinations for family vacations haven't changed much since I was a kid, but how we travel certainly has. I remember our road trip from Green Bay to Colorado Springs. Our station wagon had no air conditioning. Sweating in the backseat, my sister, Christine, and I argued vigorously.

Although large, the backseat was a border war. Social order depended on strict observance of the invisible dividing line. Chaos erupted if a stray pinky finger or kneecap crossed over. My father threatened to pull over, jerk me out of the car, and—well, he never really said what would happen. It would not have been difficult, mind you, since these days predated the era of seatbelt obsession.

The backseat was the battleground. The front was the Rand McNally command center. Maps for each state filled the vinyl chasm between my road-weary parents. They were careful only to use them when absolutely necessary, since folding them back up correctly was a task that even my architect father found challenging.

Families like my own still make summer treks to a myriad of cross-country destinations. But sweaty station wagons have given way to air-conditioned SUVs, and we all wear seatbelts. Kids still wage space wars in the back, but they are mediated now by ear buds and sundry devices. But something's missing in the front. No more paper accordions. Instead, the polite (and oddly British) voice on our GPS instructs, "Enter your destination, please." As before, it is still up to us to choose our destination before simply beginning a journey. We need to know where we are going so we can select the best route to get us there.

It's the same with storied leadership. As an intentional leader, you need to know where you want to lead me. Telling me random stories of your life or faith may entertain me. They may even inspire me, but not necessarily toward change. Ever walk out of a church service featuring a great speaker? You loved and remember the stories—but it suddenly dawns on you that you're not sure what the message was? Storied leadership requires the choosing of stories that have intentional goals.

7 The Identity Story

Years ago, my parents generously offered to take my family and my sister's family to Disney World for a week. Yes, very generous, indeed. On our first day, we all stood on Main Street in the Magic Kingdom. And it began. My sister asked, "Well, where should we go first?"

My mother responded, "It doesn't matter to us, honey. Where do you and Jay want to go?"

They looked at me. I shrugged a bit, raised my eyebrows, and scrunched my lips together, a gesture that saw their refusal to control and raised it with my noncommitment.

That's the way the Martinsons play the game of nondecision-making. Grounded in selflessness, nobody wants to come across as pushy, controlling, or insensitive. Kindness is king. Eventually decisions get made but only after everyone has been persuaded that we're all totally ambivalent and thrilled as punch to do anything, nothing, or both.

But suddenly there in the kingdom, something truly magical happened. Jeanette (the in-law!) broke rank. "Well, I'm heading to Fantasy Land, see ya!" she said, and bounced off without looking back.

Jaws dropped. Heads slowly turned. Eyes stared. *Who is that woman?*

I was torn. *Do I follow her, since I am sort of, well, married to her? But will doing so signal betrayal to my family's way of deciding, and not deciding?*

One thing was clear. If she thought she could change us, she had indeed ventured deep into fantasyland.

There are many stories just like that one. We're all committed to keeping Jeanette around, but she doesn't exactly swim by the rules set for my genetic pool. In all fairness, my sister did concede, "I like having Jeanette around because we don't have to think." A compliment? Probably not. Either way, I've not had to think for three decades. She tells me I like it.

About Us

If we could break boundaries of the space-time continuum, I'd ask each of you right now to share just one story about your family that pretty much sums them up. Everyone could do it. These are identity stories because they give insight into the identity of the person, family, organization, or culture they represent. These are our stories, *about us*.

Many corporate websites have a front-page link labeled *About Us*. In typically a paragraph or two, an organization's story is told. As an example, here's what I learned when I clicked *About Us* on the Elwood Staffing website:

> Founded in 1980, Elwood Staffing, a privately owned corporation, is a leading provider of talent-based solutions. With offices that span the United States and extend into Canada, a broad service portfolio, and a seasoned staff, we support companies through the entire employment life cycle—from attraction to retention.[1]

In forty-eight words, I have learned when their story began, who they are, what their organization is, and where they do business. More importantly, I've learned what they do and have some insight into what they value. All in forty-eight words. That's impressive. It's a concise corporate identity story. It answers the *Who are they?* question for anyone curious to know the answer before choosing to associate with them.

Corporate, as well as family, identity stories are told everywhere. Restaurants often tell these on their menus and through framed news clippings adorning their walls. One business posts its mission statement. A hospital engraves core values into granite. A grocery store lists its five "shopper promises" on drop-down banners in the aisles. A home is adorned with rub-on scripture and folksy sayings that proclaim their values. A church mission statement appears at the top of every worship service bulletin. These are all identity stories. *This is who we are.*

Self-Revelation

"Thank you for coming in today for this interview. Have a seat. Before we get started, will you tell me a little about yourself?"

I'm going to guess most of us can relate to this classic interview opener. Perhaps you've been the one asking the question. It's more than small talk. It's more than merely a warm-up before things get serious. This classic question is what we all want to know about individuals, organizations, and even larger cultures. I want to know who you are before I become your friend, date you, hire you, do business with you, or follow you on social media. I want to know more about your organization before I invest my money in it, make it my alma mater, entrust my healthcare to it, or take my family to worship in it.

Wanting us to understand the nature of his Father and the kingdom of heaven, Jesus tells stories. The nature of the parable as a story has a dual purpose—to reveal truth to those who seek it, and to conceal the truth from those with hardened hearts, who hear the story but miss the lesson. When the disciples ask him why he speaks in parables, Jesus replies, "Because the knowledge of the secrets of the kingdom of heaven has been given to you, but not to them" (Matthew 13:11). Through them, we are given images including God's mercy, forgiveness, grace, Christian love, persistent prayer, stewardship, and final judgment—to name only a few.

In dozens of simple yet poignant stories, Jesus reveals the identities of himself, his Father, the kingdom of heaven, those who would follow, and even those who would not. It's as if Jesus is saying, *This is who I am; this is what I'm about.* The choice of whether to follow, then, lies at the feet of listeners. But they know *whom* they are following.

As Christian storied leaders, communicating identity is important. Expressing our identities as sinners saved by grace communicates hope to all who listen. If our churches are communities of grace and transformation, we need to tell that story. If our members show love, mercy, and forgiveness, then that kind of good news must be told because everyone seeks narratives of hope, grace, transformation, love, mercy, and forgiveness. Remember the Monomyth? All seek heroic intervention on their cyclical journeys—resolution to conflict and sin. Other people, organizations, and substances seem to offer narrative identities of hope. Only Christ delivers. Are we telling this story?

Or do our stories only highlight activities and programs? While these can get people through the doors of our churches, we must remember that people are searching for so much more. We are all searching for something (some*one*) life-changing we cannot find elsewhere. People aren't simply seeking more information; they are seeking transformation. Do people find transformation in your church? Tell *those* stories.

Telling Our Identity Stories

The ability to lead others requires trust from others, and proving ourselves trustworthy. As individuals and churches, this begins with letting others know who we are. The small and large ways by which we do this all contribute to the construction of our identity stories.

Consider a fictitious example of Grace Church. Grace Church has a mission statement that emphasizes their commitment to bring the redeeming love of Christ to their community. That's who they are. They operate a robust food pantry, open their doors for children's sports ministries, offer career-counseling services to the unemployed, and facilitate an ongoing prison ministry. Highlighting and telling the story of someone who found hope in Christ from any of these particular ministries would offer insight into Grace Church's identity. The message of identity communicated would be consistent not only with their mission (or *who we are*) but also with the heart of Christ. Inspired by similar teachings of St. Francis of Assisi, we are reminded to "always remember to preach the gospel; if necessary, use words."

Sometimes, when I'm trying to describe what my church is like, I tell a story that perfectly captures its identity. When he was just eight years old, our son T.J. and his best friend, Josh, were playing in our backyard one spring. Little did I know they had gotten hold of the five-foot spears T.J. and I had carved to razor sharpness up at the cabin the previous summer. They began pole-vaulting with them, driving the blunt end into the ground as they ran and jumped as high as possible.

It was great fun until T.J. came down with his eye landing on the tip of one of the spears. By the grace of God, it missed his eyeball, but it sliced open his lid and severed his tear duct. There was blood everywhere.

I made just one phone call to a friend from church as we drove to the emergency room. T.J. was frightened. We were frightened. Within forty-five minutes, our senior pastor and his wife were there. Our executive pastor and wife were there. Our children's pastor was there. A member of our Sunday school class was there.

I'll always remember the image of T.J. lying on the gurney, about to be wheeled off to surgery. Pastor Cindi Schimmelpfennig held his hands, praying with him. Once he was in surgery, the visitors' attentions turned to our needs. They brought supper to us in the waiting room, which felt like a family room.

Surgery went well, and T.J. was released the next day. When we arrived home, we found food for the family and a special gift bag for T.J. that had been brought over by yet another member of our church family.

The uncertainty of that event brought fear to us as parents, but our church family converged upon us with love, support, and prayer—which is what our church *always* does. What does this single story tell you about my church? If you were looking for a church in my town and heard this story, would it make you want to come and visit?

As an individual, your storied leadership requires narrative fidelity. In other words, you can't portray an identity in Christ while living a life (secret or otherwise) contrary to that. Some situations may call for the simple sharing of your before-and-after testimonies. More often, however, storied leadership requires a more recent story that reveals some aspect of Christ's identity reflected in what he has done for you, and that may be of particular encouragement to the listener. If the listener is experiencing fear, what before-and-after story from your life can you tell that communicates God's faithfulness when you recently encountered fear? These simple, real, and current before-and-after stories serve as identity stories because they illustrate who Christ is and what Christ does. The power and proof lie in your own credibility as a leader, as a storyteller, and as a Christian. Without this narrative fidelity, our stories are, well, just talk.

Harley

Our before-and-after stories reveal the identity of Christ to others. Sometimes with unbelievers, however, our first goal is to nudge them toward our church because experiencing a faith community may be pivotal in leading them to Christ. This is where Jeanette shines. One recent summer, my family was waiting to order at the walk-up window outside Dairy Queen. The evening peace was broken by the distinctive chugging of Harley-Davidson pipes. Clad in full leather, a middle-aged couple had pulled up. As they removed their helmets, Jeanette left the line and headed straight for them.

Although she'd never actually ridden one herself, she complimented the beautiful bikes. The couple appreciated the attention drawn to the loves of their lives. Seconds later, I heard her inviting them to our church's upcoming motorcycle Sunday. It was going to be huge. Free barbecue. A motorcycle contest. Giveaways. A group ride after what would be a special worship service.

In under three minutes, Jeanette had given them a narrative of our church, communicating part of its identity, which meshed with the identity and probable needs of this couple. Jeanette offered no altars and presented no seven steps to salvation. She did not discourse with brilliant apologetics. She simply told a spontaneous, quick story that communicated plenty about our church's identity as an inclusive, caring community interested in fellowship, worship, and motorcycles. There was no need in that moment for an exhaustive story of every program and pastor; just an honest narrative that communicated who we are and an invitation to join us.

We Can't Not Communicate

As individuals and as churches, we tell identity stories all the time, sometimes intentionally. People read messages about our identity based on how we dress, what we say (or don't say), how we treat people (even when really frustrated), and how we act on the other six days of the week. Based on these things, our lives become stories that our children, coworkers, and even servers and clerks read about who we are. These unintentional messages told about our identity often have greater impact than those we choose to tell about ourselves. This is why I fear the things my children may tell their teachers and youth pastors about me! When the youth pastor asked the teens to use one word to describe their families, my daughter Rachel said, "dysfunctional." Try to do identity damage control after that one!

What about your church? How do visitors learn who you are? Is your mission statement visible and easy to understand? Are stories frequently shared that reveal the identity of your church? Are stories told in a variety of contexts and through a variety of media? Each story is different in terms of people, programs, and places. Does each contribute to the same identity embraced by your church? How well does your church tell its story? If the Lord is actively moving in the lives of those in your church, then tell that story, and tell it well.

In addition to the identity stories that churches tell intentionally, they also send unintentional messages, for better or worse. What unintentional stories does your church send? When people seek to learn about your church identity, do they visit your website, only to find outdated information? Do they look at your social media profile and find only ski trip photos, when it's now July? Do these same media offer black-and-white lists of names, schedules, and announcements, or do they tell engaging stories of personal transformation? Remember, people are not on their journeys to find schedules and announcements; they are seeking a hero—someone who can offer real change. Does radical change happen at your church? How can we know, if you're not telling the story?

What identity narrative am I reading from your physical facilities? My brother-in-law pastors a small church (runs under twenty-five) in southern Illinois. The building is old. The walls are concrete blocks. The modest fellowship hall has metal folding chairs and plastic folding tables. But here's the thing: Everything is clean. Enormous effort and pride are obviously invested in keeping this building—God's house—looking like a house of God. The grounds are well kept. Updates are made as finances provide, but in the meantime, things are maintained with such care that its message of identity is clear: This is just a building, but we respect it as a special place of worship. A clean building, however, would be a mixed message if the people weren't equally caring and welcoming, which they are. Every time we visit, we leave feeling like we've truly been in the presence of the Lord and his kingdom.

□   □   □

Have you ever received particularly great, or horrible, customer service? In either case, I bet you told someone about it. Probably many people. When at Disney World (yes, the same trip that revealed my family's identity), we were at a character brunch at our Disney hotel. Since she has hypoglycemia, Jeanette asked for a diet, caffeine-free cola. Our waiter said they had diet but not caffeine-free. He then disappeared. Moments later, he reappeared with everyone's drink in glasses on a tray.

Among the glasses was one can of soda. It was a diet, caffeine-free cola. He had left the restaurant, gone to his staff break room, and used his own money to buy Jeanette's drink from the vending machine. The fact that I'm still telling this story nearly two decades later reveals the immense power of kindness. This one story reveals not only the identity of that server but also the strong value on customer service embraced by Disney as a corporation.

What messages of identity does your church send as I drive up to it? Is the roof missing shingles? Is the landscaping overgrown? What kind of reception do I receive at the door? What about once I'm inside? Will one simply point out directions to us or actually lead us to where our children need to go? Are the bathrooms clean? I'm not looking for a country club; my community already has that. But I may assume a certain consistency between the care of the facility and the care I might receive as a person. Will people speak to me? Will the service, regardless of whatever special or out-of-the-ordinary things happening that day, still represent a consistent message with the identity of this place of worship? Will the narrative identity of your church be one that meets my Monomyth needs of love, direction, fellowship, and transformation?

Like the Disney employee, we too are leaving people with stories of our identity. What will those stories be? How can I go out of my way to live out the mission and identity of my church? Of my Lord? People are highly sensitive to incongruence—where actions don't match words. How can I relate to and love others in ways that exceed their expectations?

People are telling stories about you and about your church. What are they?

Reflect or Discuss

1. The author opens this chapter with a single story that sheds insight into the identity of his family and their dynamics. What story might similarly reveal parts of *your* family's identity?

2. To what degree does your identity reflect that of Christ? Are people seeing an image of Christ's identity by observing your life?

3. Beyond offering lists (which are important!) of programs and service times, what two or three stories could you tell about your church that would give someone insight into its identity? Would these make me want to come?

4. Some of us are intimidated by the notion of inviting total strangers to church. How can Jeanette's Harley story demonstrate how natural (and even appreciated) it can be?

5. For those who don't know Christ, the most important story we can tell is who Christ is. How can *your* before-and-after stories most directly reveal who Christ is and what he's done?

8   The Vision Story

Where there is no vision, the people perish…
—*Proverbs 29:18, KJV*

Growing up with an architect for a father had its perks. One was getting to work for him during the summers of my college years. I considered it my chief responsibility to provide wit and charm to the several architects and engineers who were being paid well to work—not to waste time joking around with me. This may be why I was relocated to the back storage room all by myself. There, however, I was given the most amazing task ever. I got to construct a 1/80 scale model of an enormous piece of property (complete with a home, outbuildings, an airstrip, and a hangar). This kept me busy and out of everyone's way for several weeks.

I also learned how to do perspective drawing, which is the art of drawing buildings as they appear in space, with lines getting closer together the farther they are from the viewer. They begin with the choice of one's standpoint, or perspective (i.e., the view of a person standing looking at it, an aerial view, or even a worm's eye view from the ground). Regardless of how it was set up, the result would offer a fairly realistic representation of the structure from that particular position, or perspective.

Clients wanted both perspective drawings and models to help them get an accurate understanding of what the building would actually look like. Untrained eyes have difficulty imagining what a structure will actually look like from a labyrinth of blue lines and tiny numbers covering page after page of blueprints. They trust the architect (sort of) but want to see it for themselves, or at least, the best representation possible. They have a lot invested; they want to see a vision of their future.

☐ ☐ ☐

I'll never forget one particular time I was driving through Chicago. My eye was caught by a billboard that read, *From where you are to where you want to be.* I thought it was catchy. Then I noticed it was advertising my own place of employment, Olivet Nazarene University. What a great statement of vision! It challenged students to imagine where they would like to be, knowing an education would be required to get there. Having that firm vision in place is the encouragement to take the first steps.

This is where identity and vision narratives differ. Identity narratives focus on who I am (or who we are). They build trust for listeners, readers, or audiences as they learn more about who we are and what we believe. They are essential for creating and sustaining a consistent narrative for us as faithful followers of Christ and as a church body of believers. Vision narratives, in contrast, focus on the future. They are about where we are going and what we want to be. We can also hold vision narratives for others—whom we believe someone could be, or the kind of impact we want our church to have in our community; from where it *is*, to where we want it to *be*.

Visions are difficult to communicate. As storied leaders, we may have a vision for ourselves, our family, our church, our community, or our nation. But what good is it if we can't communicate it? Like trying to make sense of a full set of architectural details, people may not understand an abstract vision that is not immediately available or visible. Telling a vision narrative is the equivalent of handing someone a model or perspective drawing. Like the drawings, our vision narratives strip away the minutiae of details that, though eventually important, are not critical now and may only lead to confusion. Instead, we choose an image that conveys the big picture. We need a vision that synchronizes our imaginations and evokes a range of emotional notes all from the same chord.

Big Enough to Motivate

Vision narratives inspire us to change from where we are, to where we could be. Dr. John C. Bowling, the president of Olivet Nazarene University, tells this story in his book *ReVision*:

> Some years ago as I was walking across a crowded public square, I spotted a young man coming toward me wearing a T-shirt with a slogan written on it in simple but bold letters: "Be yourself, only better." What a great thought for individuals and for institutions! Each business or organization must find—then embrace—its own identity and strive daily to be its best self.[1]

What a great illustration for how vision narratives function. We are *here*; but we can be *there*. But what kind of vision narrative can truly motivate an individual or group to push forward? Would you commit to trying my workout regime if my after photo looked only slightly different from my before photo? Probably not. If, however, the difference was significant, I would have your attention. I could even warn you of the commitments you'd need to make in terms of time, money, inconvenience, and changing some habits. But if that after photo is something you want badly enough for yourself, you're in. You want to be yourself, only *better*.

As a fourth grader, Colin Kaepernick was asked to list goals for his future. That school assignment resurfaced many years later and was reprinted in Kaepernick's hometown paper:

> I'm 5 feet, 2 inches. 91 pounds. Good athlete. I think in 7 years I will be between 6ft and 6ft 4 inches, 190 pounds. I hope I go to a good college in football, then go to the Niners or the Packers even if they aren't good in 7 years. My friends are Jason, Kyler, Leo, Spencer, Mark, and Jacob.
>
> Sincerely,
> Colin[2]

Young Colin set an ambitious and specific vision. If I had been his teacher, I would likely have chuckled and thought, *Yeah, right*. Kaepernick, however, did grow to be six feet four inches tall. In 2011, he was the fourth draft pick by none other than the San Francisco 49ers.

What is your vision for yourself? Your family? Your church? Your community? Is it big enough to motivate you? Is it big enough that there's no possible way you could accomplish it apart from total dependence on the Lord?

Of Grapes, Grasshoppers, and Gallows

Twelve spies are sent out into the Promised Land for surveillance. The bounty is great! Enormous clusters of grapes, pomegranates, and more. One problem exists. Those living there are like giants, making the spies seem like mere grasshoppers in comparison. There seems to be consensus: *We can't do it.*

But then Caleb stands. He and Joshua, together, cast a different vision that includes taking possession of the land. After all, Joshua reminds them about the people living in the land, "Their protection is gone, but the Lord is with us. Do not be afraid of them" (Numbers 14:9).

Discovering Haman's imminent plot to kill the Jews, Mordecai sends an urgent message to his cousin Esther, the queen. Although also a Jew, she has been chosen by the king without this knowledge. Mordecai casts the narrative vision that Esther should appeal directly to the king as an attempt to save the Jews. Esther questions this vision since she herself can be sentenced to death just for approaching the king without invitation. Mordecai repeats the vision, affirming it by asking, "And who knows but that you have come to your royal position for such a time as this?" (Esther 4:14).

Finally accepting the enormous vision, Esther commits to pursue it, stating her resolve: "And if I perish, I perish" (Esther 4:16).

Her courageous vision comes to fruition, and her people are spared. And the gallows constructed by Haman find an ironic purpose after all.

Two dangerously big visions that would be impossible apart from God: claiming a land run by giants and breaking culture and law by confronting the king on behalf of thousands. In each case, however, the prevailing narratives of status quo and fear are challenged with a narrative of vision. *This is where we are, but this is where we can be!* Ordinary people offer up narratives that illustrate visions of what could be. They are big enough to motivate. In this way, Caleb, Joshua, Mordecai, and Esther are all storied leaders. Their stories now, in turn, serve as vision narratives to inspire faithfulness in us today.

Outgrowing a church building is an exciting problem to have. But construction costs appear as giants to our grasshopper eyes. How can we afford it? Where will we meet and worship during construction? Former district superintendent Dr. J. Mark Barnes, from the Church of the Nazarene's North Carolina district, offers this vision story for churches needing encouragement to see their future as giant killers if they simply trust and obey:

In the early nineties, our church's vision was to sell the current property, move to a much-needed new location, and complete a million-dollar building program, debt free. We planned to move forward with this massive undertaking while continuing active community outreach and regularly scheduled revivals, paying all district and general budgetary allotments, consistently providing salary raises to staff members, participating in work-and-witness trips for world evangelism abroad, and giving 10 percent of all funds that came in for construction to our denomination's global missionary program.

Strong local lay leadership bought into the vision even though the church was in debt by more than five hundred thousand dollars. After the sale of church properties and the purchase of a parsonage for the senior pastoral family, the process began. From a human standpoint, the vision appeared doomed from the start. The church was still approximately nineteen thousand dollars in debt before the first block on the new property was laid. But God, who gave us the vision, was in charge, providing guidance, grace, strength, and money. For four years, the community and congregation saw steady progress, and the journey concluded with the dedication of a beautiful, multifunctional property that was totally free of debt.

The middle school adjacent to the building site provided space for Sunday morning worship services. The basic, U-shaped building that surrounded the ongoing construction was utilized for Sunday evening and Wednesday evening services or activities. This setup demanded creative scenarios, including live video feeds to the three rooms that would seat the most people during revivals. Most Sunday evenings, three leadership teams—prayer/announcements/testimonies, music, and preaching—ministered simultaneously in twenty-minute segments, literally crossing paths in the hallways when moving from one location to another. In spite of less than ideal circumstances, people came, and the presence of the Lord was evident.

God helped us raise a quarter of a million dollars per year. The largest gift was just under a hundred thousand dollars from the estate of one of the board members, who had been killed in a commercial airline crash. The One who birthed the vision gave grace for God's people to be generous with money, sweat equity, and prayer. Today, the building stands as a testimony to the greatness of God and the faithfulness of dedicated people who dared to trust and obey.

□ □ □

Possibly the primary function of any leader is to cast a vision for those who follow. Guiding, modeling, and pointing the way is the very act of leadership. Because it may seem vain to suggest one knows the way others should go, leaders carry a particular burden of conscience: *Are my motives pure?* A well-spoken leader could cast visions that are motivated out of selfish ambition rather than the best interests of those he leads. A coach could have her team accept her vision of winning at all costs, leading the team to accept cheating as "just part of the game."

Instead, a Christian leader needs to cast a narrative of enthusiastic encouragement. The word *enthusiasm* has its root in the Greek language, translating to "God inside" (*entheo*) and "the condition of" (*iasm*). Joshua, Caleb, Mordecai, and Esther act courageously, under the condition of having God inside. Leaders bold enough to set visions for those who follow are attempting to *encourage* (fill others with courage) with *enthusiasm* (with God inside).

Once a vision is formed, it has to be told, and retold, and done so frequently. If a church has a social media presence, the vision can be told through multimedia storytelling using websites, posts, blogs, tweets, podcasts, photos, and videos. It can be preached, taught, and reduced to a key phrase and/or symbolic image that resonates within your faith community. Expression of it can be verbalized intergenerationally. It can be the object of coloring and craft projects by children who are an integral part of any church vision. While churches benefit from effective marketing campaigns, the telling of vision stories goes beyond marketing. We market services, products, and programs. Vision stories, however, ignite and inspire us to pursue a better future. They are about people and relationships.

In addition to visions for our faith communities, storied leaders also speak vision narratives into the lives of individuals. What teacher hasn't envisioned a better future for her students than what those students held for themselves? What parent hasn't had his heart broken for a child making poor choices sure to reap ill consequences? We find ourselves thinking, *I had hoped for so much more for you.* As storied leaders, we need to put words to our hope and express a vision narrative for these individuals to encourage them to imagine a future—*themselves, only better!*

How Far Can You See?

An architect hopes her perspective drawings, models, and computer-generated images will allow clients to see into their futures and commit to the building process in the faith of what lies ahead. As a storied leader, how can you lead by replacing restrictive narratives with visions that reframe? Begin by looking backward. What biblical narratives can you draw from to inspire vision? What inspirational stories from human history help cast the vision for your desired future? What stories from your own family's or church's history need to be rediscovered and retold to renew or expand a vision?

Even with my glasses on, I can probably not make out a particular face at more than a hundred yards. At one mile on a flat road, I could possibly make out the figure of a person if I squinted and was told where to look. Our vision is limited, right? Not really. If you can see the moon, you can see roughly 384,403 miles. If you can see the sun (please don't look directly at it on my account), you can see 93 million miles. If you can (and most of us can do so with the naked eye) see lights in the night sky from the Andromeda galaxy, then you can see 2.6 million light-years. Given that each light-year constitutes 5,865,696,000,000 miles—well, this is where my math ends.

Dr. Stephen Case, assistant professor and director of Strickler Planetarium in the department of Chemistry and Geosciences at Olivet Nazarene University, explained to me that, while our eyes can see the Andromeda galaxy, "it's important to remember that that faint, fuzzy patch is the combined light of *billions* of stars. And, just like with the sun, it's taken that light some time to get here—millions of years, in fact. That's why we say we're looking back in time when we look out into space."

So how far can you see? Well, clearly the sky is *not* the limit. But, as Dr. Case reminds us, the further and deeper our vision, the more we are looking back in time. Our best narrative visions are still seen and set through the lens of the biblical truths that were first breathed millennia ago.

Reflect or Discuss

1. While we might think people prefer smaller goals to larger ones, often we need a larger vision (like Caleb and Joshua, and young Colin Kaepernick) to truly motivate us. Explain.

2. What is the vision for your church? How is its story being told in a variety of different, yet consistent and clear, ways?

3. The author suggests that vision stories are different from mere effective marketing strategies. How are they different, and how might a church benefit from both?

4. Dr. J. Mark Barnes shared with us a story he tells churches at the beginning of their building projects. How might hearing this story inspire their own vision to trust and obey? How is Dr. Barnes's credibility central to the story's power?

5. How can we lead with *enthusiasm* (with God inside)?

6. As Dr. Case reminded us, our looking forward in space often involves looking back in time. How can we tell stories from Scripture (the look back) to inspire a vision for our own futures?

9 The Counter Story

All that is necessary for the triumph
of evil is that good men do nothing.
—Edmund Burke

For the wisdom of this world is
foolishness in God's sight.
—1 Corinthians 3:19a

Fear prevails in the face of the losing battle against the Philistine army and their champion, Goliath, as recorded in 1 Samuel 17. Another battle is happening, however. There is a narrative battle going on between David, his brothers, Saul, and Goliath. In today's vernacular, we might refer to this as smack-talking. Hearing his little brother ask questions about the giant, Eliab becomes furious with David. Defining the situation, Eliab asks, "Why have you come down here? And with whom did you leave those few sheep in the wilderness? I know how conceited you are and how wicked your heart is; you came down only to watch the battle" (1 Samuel 17:28).

Eliab's narrative for David is clear and condemning: David is irresponsible, conceited, wicked, and only suited for the sidelines. Naming is powerful, and David has a choice. He can accept his brother's anti-story and the labels about himself, and go home. Or he can counter it with a narrative of his own.

David chooses to counter, and he later says to Saul, "Let no one lose heart on account of this Philistine; your servant will go and fight him" (1 Samuel 17:32). It's as if David is saying, *Oh yeah? Would an irresponsible and wicked person volunteer to fight the giant? Yeah, I didn't think so!*

But the narrative battle to define David is continued by Saul. "You are not able to go out against this Philistine and fight him; you are only a young man, and he has been a warrior from his youth" (1 Samuel 17:33). In other words, *You're not only conceited and irresponsible; you're also just a kid!* It's a game of narrative shaming at its best.

Will David finally accept the narrative definitions being imposed on him? Hardly! This time David bolsters his narrative vision (that he can overtake the giant) by citing evidence of its validity. He reads a few bullet points from his résumé: *Killed bears who threatened my sheep. Stood up to lions who got all up in my business.* Folding it back into his tunic, he then concludes, "The Lord who rescued me from the paw of the lion and the paw of the bear will rescue me from the hand of this Philistine" (1 Samuel 17:37).

He looks up. *Did I get the job?* Long pause.

He's won the narrative battle. Saul relents and lends his support to equip David.

But it's not over yet.

Goliath also wants to impose a diminishing narrative on David. "'Am I a dog, that you come at me with sticks?' And the Philistine cursed David by his gods. 'Come here,' he said, 'and I'll give your flesh to the birds and the wild animals!'"(1 Samuel 17:43–44). In the face of such a coercive narrative from this imposing figure, I would turn and run. Many of us have allowed others' narratives to bully our perceptions.

However, David confidently (perhaps stubbornly?) articulates his narrative vision for the immediate future. "You come against me with sword and spear and javelin, but I come against you in the name of the Lord Almighty, the God of the armies of Israel, whom you have defied.

This day the Lord will deliver you into my hands, and I'll strike you down and cut off your head" (1 Samuel 17:45–46).

Combating other people's imposed narratives, David offers his final counter narrative: *I will be victorious with the strength of the Lord!*

With David and with us, narratives designed to bully, diminish, contradict, or control us often come from places of cognitive dissonance. Eliab has dissonance with two conflicting thoughts: *David is my arrogant kid brother, yet he thinks he's better than us.* The result is Eliab's attempt to challenge and change David's narrative. Saul also faces dissonance: *A mere shepherd boy thinks he can do what I, a king, cannot.* He also attempts to restore consonance by presenting David with an alternative narrative. Finally, Goliath faces dissonance: *I've defeated well-armed men, yet this one approaches with a slingshot.* He too attempts to replace David's narrative of confidence with one of fear.

From places of dissonance arise rumors, misinformation, and intentionally false narratives. Original narratives often beget other narratives. Opposition to an original or asserted narrative arises, sometimes motivated to undermine it. Other times, these anti-stories arise merely out of ignorance or hearsay (like urban legends). While we can't control or stop anti-stories from emerging, leaders often counter them with additional stories that may ultimately overcome, reframe, or correct them with what Stephen Denning calls *counter stories.*[1] One obvious example is gossip. Untrue gossip may emerge about a pastor, church, denomination, or theology. Although we can declare it untrue, we as leaders may also respond with counter stories that serve to reinforce the truth. What can emerge is an eventual story that reinforces, clarifies, or even expands the original story.

Image Swapping

Kids' feet grow. That's a problem for parents with lots of kids' feet that play sports. Each season we attempt to force a too-small soccer cleat onto a too-big foot. Too bad, because the shoes are still in good shape. Light bulb! What if someone opened a local business that allowed parents to swap their too-small sporting equipment for just-right sporting equipment? I'm too late because these businesses already exist. The owner replaces that which doesn't fit with stuff that does. The dissonance (or, in this case, physical pain) is relieved.

We develop all kinds of crazy images that, well, don't fit. Images of God, images of Christians, images of ourselves, images of our church, images of our denomination, and so on. Born out of people's backstories, these images may not fit, but they wear them anyway. Some reflect hostility, hurt, and cynicism; others simply reflect ignorance. Either way, these images name, label, and define reality for them, so they hold enormous power. What if we could help swap these out for ones that did fit? Narratives hold enormous power to do just that.

To the person with a faith narrative of judgment, I could share a counter narrative that illustrates mercy and grace. To the one whose faith narrative is distorted by bitterness, I could share a counter narrative that displays forgiveness. For the boy's image of self-doubt, I can share a counter narrative that portrays confidence in Christ. To the man choked by worry about an uncertain future, I tell a counter story showing peace in an unchanging God.

An image swap starts with effective listening. I need to understand the backstory to identify the dissonance that gave rise to the anti-story. Only then can I offer a swap that fits. And hey, if the shoe fits...

Use Your Words

Your narrative has been challenged with an anti-story. Rumors are circulating about you, your family, your pastor, your church, your boss, your nation's president. If they are true, own up, correct, and change the narrative. But what if they aren't true? Naturally we can't control what others think and say. We can't become obsessed with caring about every critical comment that might arise about us or those we care about. As my mom would say, we need to have thicker skin. You were right, Mom, thank you. But we also know that leaders need the discernment to know which things to let pass and which things they cannot ignore.

For that which cannot be ignored, storied leaders rely on the power of narrative to counter anti-stories. They "confute [overwhelm or refute] the bad and extol the good," as articulated by Isocrates nearly 2,400 years ago:

> Because there has been implanted in us the power to persuade each other and to make clear to each other whatever we desire...we have come together and founded cities and made laws and invented arts... For this it is which has laid down laws concerning things just and unjust, and things base and honorable... **It is by this also that we confute the bad and extol the good.** Through this we educate the ignorant and appraise the wise; for the power to speak well is taken as the surest index of a sound understanding, and discourse which is true and lawful and just is the outward image of a good and faithful soul. (Emphasis added)[2]

Doing Good

Being good implies *doing* good. In the parable of the talents, the master condemns the wicked servant for having done nothing with what he has been given (Matthew 25:14–30).

In Ephesians 2:8–9, Paul reminds us that it is by grace we are saved, not by works. But then he emphasizes that we "are God's handiwork, created in Christ Jesus to do good works, which God prepared in advance for us to do" (Ephesians 2:10).

In Titus, we are similarly reminded that Christ "gave himself for us to redeem us from all wickedness and to purify for himself a people that are his very own, eager to do what is good" (Titus 2:14).

Part of doing good involves *defending* good. Whether they've arisen out of cynicism, disagreement, or simple ignorance, some narratives need to be countered with truth. Some examples could include:

- Someone's hesitancy to attend your church is based on rumors that it doesn't accept divorced people. You declare the rumor untrue, but it's your word against someone else's. So you offer a narrative that will hopefully counter this anti-story. You tell of your divorced friend Susan, who not only belongs to your church but also helps run the food pantry. Part of her testimony is how the church has shown her the love of Christ throughout her challenges. It's just one story, but it counters the images that led to one's dissonance.

- A coworker says he isn't interested in church or Christianity because of all the hypocrites he's experienced in churches. This hypocrisy image is common and is the point of dissonance for many. Rather than argue with or debate his narrative, you offer a different one with different images. You simply share your own story, emphasizing that you were once one of those same hypocrites. While not denying the presence of hypocrisy, you suggest that church is precisely where hypocrites should be, where they can experience the love of Christ. Further, you explain that if we refused to associate with hypocrites, we would have to avoid grocery stores, hospitals, and businesses because hypocrisy is a sin and a *people* problem, not strictly a church problem.

- Your son feels it is poor stewardship for your pastor to drive a new, upscale car. Bothered by his misconception of your pastor, you hope to replace the image with a more accurate narrative. You remind him of the time three years ago when this same pastor made several trips (fifty miles each way) to visit your son's grandfather in the hospital. For someone regularly spending this much time in his car to care for people, a reliable and comfortable car is *not* a luxury.

- Someone has grown up in a legalistic religious environment with a resulting image of God as merely a harsh judge, eager for us to step out of line. To help counter that image, you tell the biblical story of Jesus caring for the woman accused of adultery. You challenge her current image of God as harsh and vindictive with one of grace and forgiveness in the face of legalistic onlookers.

- You've come to learn there's a community perception that your church is fairly exclusive, focused only on serving its own members. With an honest inward examination, you admit that most of your focus has been on growing and discipling church families. The perception is accurate. You have not been fulfilling the part of your mission that is to serve your community. As a church, you commit to a renewed emphasis on prayer and service for your community that is designed to meet real needs. While this renewed commitment doesn't represent a verbal counter story to anti-stories, it responds with the more powerful narrative of *action*.

The frequently misunderstood concept of sanctification deserves clarification. Stories circulate about it being something that results in perfect actions, never making mistakes, or never facing temptations. We could debate the definition, or we could counter with an additional story. Dr. John Seaman, the Nazarene district superintendent for the Michigan district, has a story that does just that:

I remember a time when the Spirit of God used my son, Lauren, to convict my heart. We were living in the Ivory Coast. It was many years ago now, but I remember it like it was yesterday. Lauren was fifteen. It had been a particularly trying time, and I'd had a hectic day. I was weary and just wanted to get away for a couple of hours. Lauren and I went to the American Embassy's recreation center to watch a ball game on the embassy's satellite network.

All I wanted to do was relax, but when we arrived, the Ivorian guard at the gate was new, and he didn't recognize me. We had just gotten a used car to replace one that had been stolen, so he didn't recognize the car either. And I was frustrated because I had forgotten my membership card! So the guard really checked me out carefully. When he came back from the guard shack, logbook in hand for me to sign, even though he was just doing his job, I unreasonably found his treatment of me irritating, and I let him know in no uncertain terms how I felt about it. He opened the gate, and as we drove to a parking spot at the bottom of the hill, Lauren quietly said, "A little stressed, are we?" It may be humorous now, but at that moment, it was like a dagger thrust to my heart, and immediately I sensed not only my son's disappointment in me but God's as well.

We went to watch the game, but I couldn't enjoy it, and after a few moments I excused myself, trudged up to the guard, and told him I was sorry for the way I had acted. Later that night, before we went to bed, I apologized to Lauren too, and told him I had asked the guard to forgive me.

A sanctified heart is sensitive to the Spirit and responds *immediately* to the Spirit's convicting love. Fault, oh yes; sin, no. Had I deliberately refused to respond to the Spirit's nudge, it would have become sin. As entirely sanctified believers, our response becomes an immediate no when tempted and enticed because our heart's deepest desire is but one thing: God.

□ □ □

As missionaries, Scott and Emily Armstrong are living out the Great Commission. Yet along the way, they encounter anti-stories that require correction. One common yet inaccurate story is that Haiti can only receive missionaries, not *provide* them. Rather than debate or argue that perception, Scott responds to that anti-story with this real counter story that challenges and corrects this perception:

What's the first thing that pops into your mind when you hear the word *Haiti*? The earthquake? Poverty? Political corruption? It was one of those, right? Well, the phrase that pops into my mind is *miraculous generosity*. Countries like Haiti have been receiving missionaries for decades, but God is transforming missions nowadays into a two-way street. The missiologist Samuel Escobar calls this "missions from everywhere to everywhere." This change has been confirmed time and again by youth across the globe who are responding to God's call to cross-cultural ministry. Thus, as part of our family's ministry in Central America and the Caribbean, we issued the challenge to our countries to send their own volunteer missionaries. That's right—*volunteer*, as in, raising their own funds from their own families and churches.

We saw God work in amazing ways as he raised up youth from Mexico, Nicaragua, Costa Rica, and Guyana. Yet there was one country that everyone told us would never send a missionary, and that was Haiti. Many church leaders told us to invest our time elsewhere. "Haiti is too poor to send out," they said. As I met with the youth leaders in Haiti, I issued the challenge. It was a new concept for them, but they assured me that they were on board.

My translator during that time was a twenty-three-year-old named Kesner Absolu. My first impression of Kesner was that he lacked confidence in himself. He also was sick and, frankly, did not look at all the part of a successful missionary. So obviously I was surprised when Haiti interviewed potential candidates, and Kesner was selected.

In the following months, we trained Kesner. He had shoddy internet and had never used Skype, so this was an adventure. He required seven visas to get to the countries where the mission team would be ministering. Slowly and surely, those issues were taken care of. However, the issue of fundraising hung over our heads. Were there offerings coming in? Did people even know about Kesner and his need? Would we have to cancel his flights and admit defeat?

Two weeks before deployment, he wrote me an email (a miracle in itself). I read the joy in Kesner's words as he notified me that he had visited dozens of churches and shared his testimony. The entire amount had been raised—more than two thousand dollars. Haiti had done it.

The tears in my eyes clouded the words on the screen. I almost missed the very last part. Kesner signed his email with the following: *Kesner Absolu, First Young Haitian Missionary.*

"In the midst of a very severe trial, their…extreme poverty welled up in rich generosity" (2 Corinthians 8:2).

Choose Your Narrative Battles

My mom surely isn't the only wise mother. I'm sure yours told you to pick your battles. If so, she was right too. The war of rhetoric holds the same rules. We don't want to become reactionary people on the defensive, chasing rumors with catchy comebacks. That's not our mission or our purpose. Yet naming, labeling, and defining do have power. With them we assert our identity (*this is what I believe*) and our vision (*this is where we can be*). Using this power is called leadership. But it won't always be met with acceptance. "For the message of the cross is foolishness to those who are perishing, but to us who are being saved it is the power of God" (1 Corinthians 1:18). There are many who, in various forms and media, are willing to create the anti-story of the cross as foolishness. But remember the Monomyth? If all seek some form of hero, we know the only one able to fill that role. So, for them, the message of the cross is the power of God. It deserves being told, clarified, defended, retold, and retold, and retold yet again.

Reflect or Discuss

1. What are some common misconceptions you hear about the following, and what one or two specific stories could you offer that would counter and correct them?
    a. The Christian faith
    b. Your church or denomination
    c. Central theological concepts

2. How do these misconceptions often arise from people's backstories?

3. To what degree do we bear the responsibility of countering falsehood with truth?

4. Explain how countering misunderstandings and falsehoods with counter stories is less threatening (for us and for our listeners) than debate and argumentation.

10   The Challenge Story

This will date you (and me) a bit, I realize. But do you remember the poster from the 1970s that featured a frightened kitten hanging precariously by its front paws to a thin steel bar? The text inspired us to: *Hang in there!* That poster helped me survive open-collared silk shirts, platform shoes, bell-bottomed pants, and disco. Thanks to you, kitty, I hung in there.

As we've discussed, we tend to see our lives as narrative journeys. Ask any person what he did yesterday and he'll tell you a story of his day—complete with people, places, challenges he faced, and even how he found resolution. We see our individual days and the moments within our days as narrative journeys. They comprise struggles and problems that send us looking for solutions or a hero. Stepping back, we can also describe our lives as one large journey. We recall our past and current struggles: divorce, sickness, loss, abuse, unemployment, dissatisfaction, debt, and so on. Likewise, we can articulate our search for solutions: counseling, friendship support, self-help books, and various forms of self-medication including spending, drinking, eating, and so on.

Our circumstances differ. However, seeing our lives as journeys is a shared experience. We can all relate. We face different challenges on our journeys, but we all face them. After we come through them, we may feel confident. But at the front end of a challenge, we're not so confident. What may seem like a molehill to you may be a mountain to me.

Sometimes our challenges are common or comedic; other times they are as complicated as cancer. Regardless of their sizes and complexities, challenges become part of our narratives as individuals, as families, as churches, and as nations.

If I Can, You Can

One of the most powerful things we can do as storied leaders is to speak hope into another's narrative. The most common way we do this is by sharing parts of our own narratives to provide hope to those facing challenges similar to what we faced. The kitty poster is adorable and has probably inspired millions who have found themselves precariously dangling from chin-up bars, steel trusses, branches, or telephone lines. But if I'm going through divorce, I find little comfort in the cat's conflict. I need hope that I can make it through this challenge. I want someone who understands, someone who's been there. Sharing a narrative that communicates empathy (not merely sympathy) can inspire the hope I need with the message: *If I can, you can.*

The source of our best challenge stories, then, is our own experience. I was looking for a new exercise routine a few months ago. My son T.J. suggested a particular video series he had used. I was doubtful. I had heard horror stories about how difficult this series was. "No," he reassured me, "you can do this, Dad." He explained his experience with it, including the early soreness as well as the eventual, desired results. "Really, it's not that bad. I know you can do it." I trusted my son. He wasn't trying to sell me something; his only motivation was caring about me and wanting to help. He knew my abilities better than most. He had been through this routine personally. Encouraged to go for it, I committed. And, for the record, I made it through without skipping a single day—because my son believed I could.

Many of us have made it through life challenges because of teachers, pastors, coaches, parents, and friends who have essentially said, *If I could, so can you.* Motivating one through a challenge can be done in ways similar to the North Wind and the Sun from chapter 1. If we possess the authority to do so, we may force someone into compliance or submission. But even if we do have that authority, many leaders choose to motivate in the manner of the Sun, encouraging us to act without force. Stories do this. If I can see myself in your story of personal challenge, I can likewise see myself experiencing the same outcome you did.

If we don't have (or at the moment can't recall) a personal narrative that we think will be connect with the listener, the second-best option is to share someone else's story. A while ago, my friend Dr. Michael Taylor was preaching on the subject of giving. As an illustration, he told them my son Tad's story.

Over a course of many months, Tad had saved his money: birthday money, all his allowances, and money from odd jobs like leaf raking. He even asked the Easter Bunny for cash instead of candy. Finally he met his goal of one hundred dollars. We took his wadded-up bills and coins to the bank one Saturday so he could hold one crisp Franklin in his hands. He brought it with him the next day to Sunday school and handed it to his teacher, Mrs. Clupper. He said he wanted it to go to Jesus.

You can see why Dr. Taylor chose to tell this story to his congregation. Instead of a PowerPoint list of income and expenses, or a list of the many verses in Scripture about giving, or heavy-handed guilt or shaming rhetoric, Dr. Taylor chose a story. An ordinary boy with normal, little-boy, materialistic desires instead set his priorities on sacrificial giving to support the work of the Lord. The challenge message was clear: *If a little boy can realign his priorities, so can we!*

History provides endless sources of challenge stories. For example:

- *Abraham Lincoln.* For the person who's tempted to give up. Lincoln lost the election for state legislature in 1832. Although he won state legislature in 1834, he was defeated in his bid to be speaker in 1838, and to be elector in 1840. He lost his run for Congress in 1843. He won in 1846 but lost reelection in 1848. He lost runs for Senate in both 1854 and 1858. In 1856, he was defeated for the nomination of vice president. In 1860, he was elected president of the United States of America. Hearing this story forces me to reinterpret my own loss narratives. Message received: *Lincoln didn't give up; neither should I.*

- *Helen Keller.* For those facing major obstacles that could leave them feeling helpless and hopeless. At nineteen months of age, Keller contracted an illness that left her both deaf and blind. With the aid of twenty-year-old teacher Anne Sullivan, Helen learned to understand signs, braille, and even speech by touching a speaker's lips. She was the first deaf and blind student ever to receive a bachelor's degree. She became an international champion for those with disabilities, traveled broadly, and met thirteen U.S. presidents. Message received: *If I can't remove the barriers I face, I can go around them to find places of meaningful contribution.*
- *George Washington Carver.* For the person who faces large challenges while feeling disadvantaged by a lack of material resources. Born into slavery in Missouri, Carver was a sickly child, unable to do the field work required of others. Forced to stay around the house, he busied himself with gardening, earning a reputation for being good with plants. Due to his race, he was at first denied public school and, later, entrance to college. After his experimentation with plants on a homestead of land, he was finally accepted into Iowa State Agricultural College, where he became the first black student and, eventually, the first black faculty member. Despite the dozens of agricultural innovations and national honors he received, the tombstone of this strong Christian reads: "He could have added fortune to fame, but caring for neither, he found happiness and honor in being helpful to the world." Message received: *Regardless of where I begin and what I have, God can use the gifts he's given me to accomplish his will.*

God Can

The best challenge stories are those that make it clear that the person featured in the story could not have overcome the challenge apart from the strength of the Lord. I could tell my son not to feel discouraged if he doesn't make the varsity basketball team because even Michael Jordan faced the same dilemma. But my son could also remind me that Jordan's success thereafter was probably due to being six feet six inches tall and having a six-foot-nine-inch wingspan (fingertip to fingertip), which makes this story a little less comparable. And my son would be right. The best challenge stories are those that feature ordinary people whose challenges could clearly not have been accomplished without the help of the Lord.

For this reason, the best challenge stories are still found hanging in our own autobiographical closets. Since my wife and I are parents of an internationally adopted child, people who are considering the same process often talk with us. They often have full hearts but empty pockets. International adoption is an expensive challenge, to be sure. We simply tell our own story. We were an ordinary family with nowhere near the available funding. It was our mountain-sized challenge. We decided from the onset that we would not ask for money. No online or in-person fundraising. Instead, we prayed that God would provide through the provision of extra work.

Over the next eighteen months, God did just that. Jeanette and I both received night classes to teach. I started a small art business that God blessed enormously. Every morning from 4:00 a.m. until 8:00 a.m. I sat at my board, drawing my fool heart out. Local projects came in as well as ones from several states away. I wish I had space here to tell some of the miraculous ways God provided during that season because there are so many stories! When the time came for the required funding, we had it. We had to be obedient, but it was only through God's flood of faithfulness that our mountain was moved. This story is a good challenge story for those considering international adoption because it highlights God's faithfulness in the lives of ordinary people facing the same challenge. *We can't, but God can!* Whom do you know who could find encouragement from your stories of God's faithfulness?

We've all faced a mountain-sized challenge. It looks enormous, and we look really small. In such times, people may feel discouraged if focusing on their own weaknesses. This is precisely the time, however, when a listener needs a challenge story that gives evidence of the Lord's strength being perfect in our weakness. When someone is feeling discouraged about a particular challenge, Stephanie Meads, a graduate of Olivet Nazarene University, shares this story:

"I will go to college someday," I would tell Jane Dyer as she gave me rides to Roxana Church of the Nazarene. To many, that is a realistic ambition. To those who knew the situation of this "bus kid," however, it seemed like little more than a dream.

My mother died when I was just nine months old. I lived with my loving grandmother, who raised me on just six hundred dollars a month. I remember once getting a Christmas present but never birthday presents. Money was just too tight. I worked from the time I was eleven, at the library and doing odd jobs for people.

I suffered abuse for several years at the hands of a relative. But one day when my abuser had locked me out of the trailer in the cold, I sat on the steel steps. I distinctly remember looking across a field and feeling God holding me, letting me know that someday this would all be okay.

During my junior year of high school, I was able to get a ride with a local church to attend Red Carpet Days—an annual event for teenagers held by Olivet Nazarene University. There, I decided I would somehow attend Olivet. I started praying and believing.

I had to fill out my own financial aid applications, and the government thought I had made a mistake since our income was reported as so low.

I was accepted at Olivet, and despite all the financial hurdles, God provided, and I was going to college! But even traveling the four hours to campus was difficult. Someone from my home church gave me a train ticket to Dwight, where my campus recruiter—Tony Fightmaster—picked me up and drove me to my dorm. God had again provided.

During college, I worked full-time to pay my bills, sometimes leaving me with only ten dollars a month. But God met my needs. The wife of a dorm's resident director was from my home church. She invited me to do my laundry in their apartment. My supervisor at work was Carol Maxson—and while we cleaned a manufacturing plant at night, Carol regularly encouraged me with godly wisdom and Scripture. She was raising three boys by herself, finishing her degree, and working nights. If God had provided for Carol, he would provide for me too!

I'll never forget the day my pastor had me stand as he told the congregation, "We all hoped it would happen. We prayed it would happen. And it did happen. Yesterday, Stephanie graduated from college!" I received a standing ovation.

There's never been a financial challenge that hasn't been met in my life. While college was an enormous one, God has continued to faithfully meet all of my family's needs. He often even meets our wants, just to show off. That's my whole life.

None of the circumstances in my life have been a surprise to God. I just have to let him work it all to his glory.

The Lord moved mountains to get me to college. There, I met my godly husband, and together we've raised three wonderful children—one of whom recently felt a call to missions to fight human trafficking. The truth of it is that I could have done none of this by myself. And if God can do it for me, God can do it for you.

NFL chaplain LaMorris Crawford shared a challenge story with me. During his first chapel service with his team, he wanted to share with them that adversity was part of the process in fulfilling God's purpose for their lives. He also wanted them to know that God is not a respecter of persons, and that God is in the life-changing business. Here is the story LaMorris told the players that day:

On the south side of Chicago in a housing project, a boy was born into a life of extreme poverty, crime, and drugs. He never met his father, and his mother was shot and killed in a violent fight when he was only ten months old. His family was in constant survival mode, so at a young age, this boy began selling drugs and joined a gang. Academics weren't a central focus in his home, but he chose to go to school to play basketball; there, he found his identity on the court. The more he played, the better he became.

After barely completing his primary years of school, he found himself in the ninth grade, 5 feet 4 inches tall, 120 pounds, and trying out for his basketball team at a school of 2,500 students. But his height, weight, and the competition didn't matter to him, and he earned his spot on the team. Senior year came, and he was offered multiple scholarships, but his ACT scores didn't pass the minimum requirements, shattering his dreams. All at once he wasn't sure of who he was without basketball.

At the age of nineteen, he knew something had to change, or his decisions would lead to jail, poverty, or death. He asked Jesus Christ to reveal himself. In that moment, the young man was new. Everything about him changed. His desire to play basketball decreased, and his desire to learn more about the one who saved his life increased. He decided it was time to rewrite his heritage.

The young man worked three jobs to put himself through community college, then through undergrad and graduate school. He became the first person in his family to earn a degree, ever. During this time in his life, he recognized the passion he had for professional athletes. He wanted to help them become more than their game. He stands in front of you today because God changed who he was yesterday. I am the boy who became this man.

Together, We Can

We use storied leadership to encourage people through their personal challenges. We can find courage to face individual challenges from others' stories. We don't, however, want to send the message that we—as individuals—can accomplish what requires the full body of believers. Some of our most effective challenge stories, therefore, emphasize overcoming challenges with the help and support of a network of believers. This could include the help we've received from pastors, professionals, small groups, mentors, accountability partners, our families, and close friends. These stories affirm the truth for listeners that they indeed cannot do it alone; *it takes the full body.*

In addition, we need the power of story to encourage groups facing challenges. Our best attempts at igniting the unified will of a group often utilize story. We're all familiar with Dr. Martin Luther King Junior's "I Have a Dream" speech, delivered on August 28, 1963, at the March on Washington. He needed to inspire his national audience in the face of their enormous racial challenge. Before reaching the more frequently quoted sections, vividly painting his dreams, King first offered a narrative invoking Lincoln and the lack of progress one hundred years later:

> Five score years ago, a great American, in whose symbolic shadow we stand today, signed the Emancipation Proclamation. This momentous decree came as a great beacon light of hope to millions of Negro slaves who had been seared in the flames of withering injustice. It came as a joyous daybreak to end the long night of their captivity.

> But one hundred years later, the Negro still is not free. One hundred years later, the life of the Negro is still sadly crippled by the manacles of segregation and the chains of discrimination. One hundred years later, the Negro lives on a lonely island of poverty in the midst of a vast ocean of material prosperity. One hundred years later, the Negro is still languished in the corners of American society and finds himself an exile in his own land. And so we've come here today to dramatize a shameful condition.

Sharing this story established that an enormous challenge still existed. Only then did King use personal narrative to inspire listeners to believe this challenge *could be overcome*:

> Let us not wallow in the valley of despair, I say to you today, my friends.

> So even though we face the difficulties of today and tomorrow, I still have a dream. It is a dream deeply rooted in the American dream.

> I have a dream that one day this nation will rise up and live out the true meaning of its creed: "We hold these truths to be self-evident: that all men are created equal."

I have a dream that one day on the red hills of Georgia, the sons of former slaves and the sons of former slave owners will be able to sit down together at the table of brotherhood.

I have a dream that one day even the state of Mississippi, a state sweltering with the heat of injustice, sweltering with the heat of oppression, will be transformed into an oasis of freedom and justice.

I have a dream that my four little children will one day live in a nation where they will not be judged by the color of their skin but by the content of their character.

I have a *dream* today!

I have a dream that one day, down in Alabama, with its vicious racists, with its governor having his lips dripping with the words of interposition and nullification; one day right there in Alabama, little black boys and black girls will be able to join hands with little white boys and white girls as sisters and brothers.

I have a *dream* today!

I have a dream that one day every valley shall be exalted, every hill and mountain shall be made low, the rough places will be made plain, and the crooked places will be made straight, and the glory of the Lord shall be revealed, and all flesh shall see it together.[1]

King's speech inspired his twentieth-century audience to believe that the enormous racial challenge could be overcome, with the clear message of *together, we can*. As storied leadership works, his speech (in whole and in selected parts) is now used as a narrative in and of itself by contemporary speakers to motivate their twenty-first-century audiences in the ongoing challenge of racial equality.

When our churches face challenges, we can invoke the power of story to assert or remind members of our shared identity, or to unite them toward a common vision. As with individuals, the types of narratives with the most power to inspire hope in the face of challenge are often autobiographical, from the life of the church itself. My therapist wife tells me that sometimes a marriage therapist will ask troubled couples to recall stories from their early years that illustrate what they initially loved about each other. As with these couples, sometimes our churches need to be reminded of where we've come from and the things we've overcome to get here. We need to be reminded of our first love, Christ, within whom no challenge is too great. We need to be reminded of the endless array of great challenge narratives from the Bible. The underlying message of such narratives remains clear: *Together, with God, we can.*

Reflect or Discuss

1. When you have been discouraged from facing a mountain in your own life, whose challenge stories have been a source of encouragement for you?

2. Although hearing another's challenge story doesn't change our immediate circumstances, how does it function as a powerful form of leadership for us?

3. Think of an example from your own life that you could use as a challenge story illustrating, *We can't, but God can.*

4. The author lists some challenge stories from American history. What other historical or biblical challenge stories have you found particularly encouraging?

5. While many challenge stories focus on individual achievement, why are "together, we can" challenge stories particularly important?

6. What are some "together, we can" stories from your own life that would encourage another to seek and accept help from others?

11   The Change Story

In the fall of 1982 as a freshman in college, I needed to select a major, and I had an epiphany: I liked listening to music. *Ergo*, I'd become a music major! Sheer brilliance. But then I found myself in a class called Music Theory. And that was pretty messed-up stuff. I noticed that nothing in there was going to help me write cool love songs that would bring me fame and fortune. Apparently others were noticing that I wasn't noticing what I probably should have noticed. So I was summoned into the office of Dr. Harlow Hopkins, who served as chairman for the division of music.

There, he kindly and gently observed my lack of proficiency in anything related to music. He then told me he was going to let me find a major better suited for me. *What? Did he just drop me from the music major?* Yes. Yes, he did. Did it hurt? Yes, temporarily. Did it harm me? No, it did not. Soon thereafter I found myself in the English and communications department—two subjects that came easily to me and that I could use to build on my strengths. Looking back, I can't thank Dr. Hopkins enough for caring enough to confront me with the truth. That confrontation is the reason I'm in a field I thoroughly enjoy today.

Throughout my tenure as a professor and department chairman, I've told that story at least a dozen times, and while you may have chuckled at my misfortune therein, it isn't usually met with laughter— because I tell it to students whom I've discerned will not make it in my department. I tell it to students who lack the fundamental abilities required to succeed in a major related to English or communications. I tell it because I'm hoping to *inspire change*—in this case, a change of major. Since the details of the story are strikingly familiar to the student seated across from me, he cannot help but see himself in it. He cannot help but see me as Dr. Hopkins. As such, the intent of the story is that he will transfer the difficult lesson I had to learn into his own life. Further, I hope he'll see my motivation as ultimately loving, even if my actions cause temporary pain.

The change story is perhaps the most important of all the stories. If leadership is the intentional act of guiding or influencing others for their well-being, then nowhere is this done more directly than in the change story. The change story is designed to engage a problematic aspect of a person's own narrative, challenging him or her toward adopting a new one.

Syllogistically Speaking

When shared with someone who trusts us, a story can have enormous impact and potential for change. Our ordinary stories from our ordinary lives carry power. The explanation for this power dates back before the time of Christ. Early Greek and Roman rhetoricians Plato and Aristotle taught the art of persuasion, a fundamental component of which was the logical syllogism. Change stories, in their simplest form, often reduce to a syllogism designed to help a listener arrive at the speaker's intended conclusion. Here's the classic illustration of how a syllogism works:

A. All men are mortal (the basic premise).

B. Socrates was a man (the specific observation).

C. Therefore, Socrates was mortal (the drawn conclusion).

You may have heard it elsewhere, in different terms that convey the same point: *If A equals B and B equals C, then A equals C.* Let's look at an example of a change story similar to one we might actually use. Let's assume Steve's friend has been diagnosed with cancer and is experiencing anxiety over the accompanying uncertainty. Steve, having previously faced cancer himself, wants to help his friend find the same peace and trust that he found in the Lord. So he shares his story with his friend. Listening to Steve, the friend's internal conversation follows the basic syllogistic form or, what we might call simply connecting the dots:

A. Steve faced the uncertainty of cancer, yet the Lord gave him comfort and peace (basic premise).

B. Like Steve, I'm facing the uncertainty of cancer (specific observation).

C. Since Steve found comfort and peace in the Lord, *then so can I* (the drawn conclusion, which represents a change).

The Trust Transfer

For a syllogism to be persuasive, we must first believe, or trust, the basic premise—which, in our case, is the person's story. Second, we must see our own experience as similar to the experience of the person telling the story. If these two basic conditions are met, our mind is nudged toward a conclusion: *Christ can likewise change my life.* Despite our weird obsession with viral videos, karaoke, and reality TV, humans are profoundly rational beings. Because we are rational, we make a trust transfer. If I trust you, I trust your story. If it happened to you, it could happen to me too.

Further, effective tellers of change stories don't usually spell out the conclusion for the listener. It is more powerful for listeners to actively draw the conclusions for themselves. Delivering only the first part of the syllogism and allowing the listener to fill in the rest is what Aristotle called the *enthymeme.* Many pastors employ a similar homiletic approach of induction, articulated by the late Fred Craddock and others. Instead of passively waiting to be given a conclusion, listeners are engaged and actively draw the conclusions for themselves.

Specifically, Craddock suggests that, as storytellers, we are doing more than telling stories; we are evoking stories within others:

> The mark of a good story is when its listeners begin to say, 'You know, when you were talking, I was thinking of when I was once home on the farm.' Now you are stirring the stories and the stories are coming out and you are invoking the stories… Good storytelling speaks for the congregation and evokes their own stories.[1]

Consider a few additional examples that illustrate the rational way our brains inductively reach conclusions upon hearing change stories from trusted sources:

1. Jill's teenagers put her to the test, but the Lord provided wisdom and patience (the story told).
2. I've got teenagers putting me to the test (my own thought/specific observation).
3. Perhaps the Lord can give me wisdom and patience (my drawn conclusion).

1. Mike's life was consumed with worldly possessions until the Lord showed him that all he needed was God (the story told).
2. My own obsession with possessions has left me unsatisfied (my own thought/specific observation).
3. Perhaps the Lord can become the source of my satisfaction (my drawn conclusion).

1. Ann's inability to forgive imprisoned her until she surrendered her hurt to the Lord (the story told).
2. My inability to forgive is like a prison to me (my own thought/specific observation).
3. Perhaps the Lord can take my hurt and set me free (my drawn conclusion).

1. Jorge was cynical due to hypocrisy until he shifted his focus from people to God (the story told).
2. Much of my cynicism is due to so much witnessed hypocrisy (my own thought/specific observation).
3. Perhaps my dependence has also been on people instead of God (my drawn conclusion).

The word that probably bothered you the most in those examples is the word perhaps. I used that word because the story itself doesn't *cause* change. Stories aren't New Age, mystical, magical, weird, manipulative, or psycho-babble. Rather, your story can inspire one toward Christ, who *can* make the change.

An appropriate story can simply spark a necessary internal conversation of questions: *How can I achieve this same comfort? How can I surrender my hurt to the Lord?* With any luck, they'll ask the questions out loud. To you. And you'll be glad to tell them how. But it's important to realize that stories aren't silver bullets in the guns of our communication holsters. Although that would be awesome, we don't just fire off a story and gallop away into the sunset after dramatically saying, "I guess my work here is done!"

Your Story, But Not about You

It is not easy to tell an effective change story. If it's my story, I know all kinds of details that I find fascinating. These details, however, start to make the story more about me than about inspiring change in you. If my listeners get bogged down following me along tangents and rabbit trails, they are less likely to find themselves in my story. Their minds are too busy trying to sort out the details. This is where it gets tough for many of us. These are our stories; we know and appreciate all the details. But, for listeners to see themselves in the story, we have to use the delete key and start chopping unnecessary details. It's your story, but it's not *about* you.

Stephen Denning asserts that effective change stories are essentially springboard stories told in minimalistic form. They inspire listeners to find themselves in the story then springboard them to a conclusion.[2] In minimalistic form, an effective change story first needs to be true. *This happened to me.* Second, it establishes a brief context. When and where did the story take place? As narrative beings, listeners' minds seek those details for narrative validity. Third, the protagonist should be similar to the listener in some way; otherwise, there won't be strong identification. Fourth, only bare bones details are provided, lest the listener become more interested in extraneous and distracting issues. Finally, the story should make it clear what would have happened had the protagonist—usually the speaker—not made the change.

Consider my story that I've shared with students who need to change their major. First, it is true. It did happen to me. Second, it reveals a time and a place. It was the fall of 1982 in a college professor's office. Third, the protagonist is similar in some way to my intended listener. The protagonist in the story is a college student. Fourth, it contains only bare bones details, sparing the listener information about other majors I declared, other music classes I was failing, funny stories from freshman year, and so on. These would consume the listener's mental space required for imagining himself or herself in the story and reaching a conclusion. Finally, the story makes the preferred choice— finding a new major—clear, as well as the undesirable alternative—to remain frustrated in a major that is ill-suited to the person's strengths.

People Deserve Better

What drives the creation of a new ministry or program? How much of a need exists for it? Further, how do we convince others of its need? Dr. Dan Boone, president of Trevecca Nazarene University, shares of a time when the church he was pastoring faced this issue. They had grown from 850 to 1,300 in a short period of time. The weight of pastoral care had outgrown the capacity of the handful of staff pastors. They began a small group ministry designed for discipleship and care-giving. Some felt negative toward the move. Programmatic explanations failed. The thing that turned the corner and inspired change for the congregation and staff was this simple, true narrative that Dr. Boone (with the permission of those in the story) shared from the pulpit:

It was a Wednesday night prior to fall break. The service was deeply meaningful with a time of altar prayer at the end. As people lingered, I was approached by two college students. The first shared that she had just received news of the death of her mother and had packed her car to head home. She saw the lights on in the church and stopped in to request prayer. I stopped and prayed with her for traveling mercies and for the process of grief that was just beginning.

As she walked away, the other student approached me with tears in her eyes. Her parents had separated during her first semester at college, and she would be leaving the next morning to go home. The awkwardness of facing her father, and knowing about his affair, weighed heavy on her heart. I prayed with her, asking for God's wisdom and timing. Both students were new to me. I conversed with several other people who had been praying for specific needs then went home feeling tired at the end of a long day.

The students left for break and would not be back in church until the following Sunday, some ten days later. I knew neither of these students personally, but I prayed for them both a few times over the coming week. About two weeks later, I saw one of the students and approached her to see how she was doing in the wake of her parents' separation. My first words were, "How is your mother doing?"

Unfortunately, this was the student whose mother had died, not the one whose parents had separated. Her immediate, tearful reply was, "You don't even remember that my mother died."

I tried my best to explain my crossed identity, but even I was not satisfied. I knew in that moment that neither student had received the kind of care they needed and that, given our current care system, never would.

It matters to me, to you, and to God that people who attend our church receive better care than this. This is the motivation behind our small group program—that people know and are known by a circle of friends who will be there for them in the difficult moments of life.

Dr. Boone's story functions as a change story. It is a true story. It happened directly to him. It offers a specific context. It happened Wednesday night before college fall break. The story is short and effective; it doesn't go overboard with explaining the similarities in the appearances of the two young women (if such existed), and the storyteller doesn't go into all the *other* details that made his life hectic and stressful over that ten-day period, possibly contributing to a memory lapse when he saw one of the students later on. As the storyteller, Dr. Boone is the protagonist, and we cringe when we imagine ourselves in his awkward shoes. Two clear choices are presented as a result of the story: Keep the current, inadequate system, and people will be hurt; or change to a structure that allows for the provision of adequate care. Some change stories only show the protagonist making the right decision, forcing us only to *imagine* the negative consequence. This story, however, functions especially well because we see and feel the pain that actually resulted from not having the program in place soon enough. The congregation accepted the change.

Dr. Boone's change story was effective in motivating change in an entire group of people. In this vein, new leaders can capitalize on the power of narrative to inspire change in the organizations they are called to lead. In his inauguration speech as president of Bethel College in the fall of 2013, Dr. Gregg Chenoweth addressed the challenge to inspire new institutional priorities for all fifty diverse work units at Bethel. He wanted to make a strong institution even stronger. According to Dr. Chenoweth, his desired effect was to shift from casually looking into the future to intently seeing a compelling one. To be sure, he articulated a list of specific priorities he wanted the university to adopt, but to inspire a change in mindset, he *first* told a story:

Looking at what *is*, is a different task than seeing what *might* be. Niall Ferguson understands this. In his book *Civilization*, he tells how two leaders from two different countries had different eyes.

First, Emperor Yongle of the Ming Dynasty in fifteenth-century China commissioned a crew of 28,000 sailors to "go to barbarian countries and confer presents on them to transform them by displaying our power." He thought parading China's inventions might curry favor. In some cases, it worked. The sultan of Kenya was so impressed that he paid Yongle tribute by giving his delegation a giraffe. When Yongle received it, his theory was confirmed. He believed he had been given a gift of unsurpassing value. He hailed it as the mythical unicorn. So the international gift exchange worked! Everybody had cool stuff to look at. It's good to be the king!

Meanwhile, a few thousand miles away, King Manuel of Portugal had a different idea altogether. He put Vasco da Gama in command of four small ships. Their instruction was to create new ports to establish trade where it had never existed before. So when da Gama's little fleet docked at Macau, China—at that time an out-of-the-way wasteland with nothing to look at—the first thing he did was erect a gate that said, *Dread our greatness! Respect our virtue! The City of God in China.* Da Gama saw something where there was nothing to look at. He eventually strung together trading posts in Lisbon, Africa, Arabia, India, and, of course, China.

While we wouldn't endorse all of da Gama's methods—in fact, one historian said he liked to get his retaliation in first!—you have to give it to the guy. One emperor wanted to look at inventions. The other had nothing to look at. But he could see something yet to be.

Notice the key elements of an effective change story? It offers a specific time and place, and has two protagonists. Through the emperor of China and the king of Portugal, listeners are presented with two alternative methods of instituting change: Demonstrate power by forcing others to look, or display an assertive willingness to see things that *could* be. The story makes it clear which alternative is superior by citing eventual success. Lastly, the story is minimalistic. It isn't cluttered with extraneous details about fifteenth-century China, Portugal, or the two contrasting leaders. The storyteller's goal is not to show off his historical knowledge. Such details could quickly distract listeners from reaching the intuitive conclusion of, *We need to stop looking at what is and begin to see what could be.*

Offering up an appropriate story is like handing someone bread rather than stones. But, as Jesus reminds us in the New Testament, we cannot live on bread alone. Or on stories. Individuals and congregations will often have questions that require clarifications, explanations, or even the honest response of, "I don't know." They may even choose to keep their internal conversations *internal*. They may not wish to talk further at all, but the bread has been delivered. Change stories do not always result in change. Even if they do, the change isn't always immediate. Often we have to let the bread we've offered continue to rise and bake on its own.

Reflect or Discuss

1. Recall an instance where another's story inspired you toward change. What made that story so effective for you?

2. Like the author's college major story, what stories do you have that illustrate key turning points in your life and could be used to inspire another toward change?

3. The principle of the trust transfer implies that we have enormous potential to influence those who trust us. In your life, who trusts you most? In what areas of their lives could they most benefit from growth and change?

4. Be honest. In the telling of change stories, how often do you complete the syllogism for listeners rather than allow them to reach their own natural conclusions? How might that actually weaken the impact for them?

5. If we are truly sharing our stories to inspire change in others, the author urges us to use the delete key. Following the minimalistic form, how do we decide which details we keep and which we delete?

SECTION FOUR

TELLING STORIES WELL

I'm married to a rabid Red Sox fan. Jeanette has Boston Red Sox stuff everywhere. I'm fine with baseball, but I'm from Green Bay, where a different sport is king. Jeanette not only watches Red Sox baseball; she also talks it. She rattles off names, stats, acronyms (DH, ERA, ABs) and unfamiliar terms (the green monster, can o' corn, suicide squeeze, Yawkey Way). I nod along sympathetically to maintain marital bliss, but I'm not following. Sometimes we know so much about a subject that we have a hard time speaking the same language as the one who does not know the things we know. Effective communication requires connection. Knowing a lot about a subject can make connection more difficult.

Growing up on an eighty-acre farm in Denmark, Wisconsin, was great fun. We had several horses, bantam chickens, and barn cats. Our favorite animal, however, was Jodie, our faithful collie. She spent as much time outside as in. But the biggest problem with having a long-haired dog running across eighty acres of land came from the smallest of sources—the burdock plant. Sometimes called the hitchhiking plant, hundreds of these marble-sized dried blooms will latch onto pant legs and especially the fur of long-haired dogs. In fact, the burdock blooms led Swiss mountaineer George de Mestral to invent Velcro after he pulled hundreds of tiny hooks and burrs from his own dog's fur.

In their book *Made to Stick*, brothers Chip and Dan Heath refer to the *curse of knowledge*.[1] Their point is that sometimes we know so much about a topic, we have difficulty communicating about it. Effective communication is a lot like burdock; it makes a connection and sticks. As storied leaders, we harness the power of narrative to serve as hooks that will connect with the heads and hearts of listeners. The problem some of us face when trying to communicate the gospel, however, is that, like Jeanette's Red Sox obsession, sometimes we know too much to make these connections effectively. The result is that we use terminology others don't understand. Our abstract spiritual metaphors make sense to us but not to new believers. Or we only construct an argument of rational points, when the problem lies in the heart. Or we try to cover Genesis to Revelation in one sitting. The result? Nothing sticks.

12 Adapt

Social media is filled with funny videos that gently poke fun at our frequent use of religionese. These videos are often titled something like "Dumb Things Christians Say." I dare you to watch some of these and not laugh. They're funny because they carry some truth. Language matters. Theological concepts matter profoundly. The point isn't to give these up or dumb them down. As with any other effective communication, we need to talk about faith in ways that stick.

A person can be saved in an instant, accepting Christ's forgiveness of sins and salvation. There is a process, however, of learning the grammar of faith. This is often a highly social process, being discipled and nurtured in the context of a Christian community. By reading, studying, and discussing the Bible within a community of believers, our theological lexicon grows. Words like *justification*, *redemption*, *sanctification*, and *Eucharist* become grounded into our deeper understandings of faith. But to an unbeliever or a new believer, these make as much sense as Yawkey Way, can o' corn, HRs, and the green monster do to me.

As storied leaders, we can use the power of narrative to adapt complex ideas to the needs and current understandings of our listeners. These adaptations often utilize narrative tools, including concrete language, metaphors, similes, and analogies.

Concrete Language

Effective storytelling hinges on being able to speak concretely rather than abstractly. Unfortunately, some of us know too much about a given topic to explain it plainly to someone less familiar. Therefore, we often speak in generalities and highly abstract language that makes sense to us but not to our listeners. They are often left either unsure of what we meant, or assuming we meant something that we definitely did not mean.

Illustrating how we first must be concrete before moving on to abstractions, Kate Mead, a wife and mother of two, shares this example of communicating with her young son:

When my three-year-old son ends up knocking over the toys his sister is playing with or hitting her, I use the words, "Be kind." However, I am able to do this because, many times in the past, I have explained to him that we need to be kind by playing gently with the toys someone else is using, by not hitting, not yelling, et cetera. After consistently teaching this, I've been able to use a simpler, abstract instruction, only because I have explained the concept concretely many, many times before, inside a consistent relationship. He is aware of my direction because we have been over it before.

There are times when I still need to clarify those words, explaining what new action of his is inappropriate, but this just further expands the definition of the words, "Be kind." He is learning many things that kindness encompasses because concrete understanding can lead to abstract understanding. Eventually, I hope to teach him to think deductively so he can decide on his own whether a particular action is kind or unkind.

Some other examples could include:
- A father tells his son that he needs to "be more respectful." This instruction, however, is too general and abstract. Based on whatever prompted this message, he could tell his son that he needs to be more respectful toward his mother by no longer interrupting

her and rolling his eyes when she is talking to him. Further, he needs to respond to her requests immediately, rather than simply saying he'll do something but not doing it until she feels forced to tell him a second or third time.

- Instead of merely telling a friend that he should visit our church because "it's really awesome and like a big family," which is too general, we could say, "It is a group of about 120 people who pray for each other, often gather for social events together, visit one another in the hospital, and always seem to be there for support when someone needs it. When I was taken to the ER last year from my accident, my pastor and five people from church were there within an hour while another couple took care of my children until I was released that evening. They even brought over meals the following week!"

- Instead of saying to a new believer that we need to "daily die to ourselves," which is an abstract concept one will learn when more mature in the faith, we could be a lot more specific and concrete by saying that we need to "daily remember the sacrifice Christ made for us. Because he forgave us, we should not return to the sinful people we used to be. We can daily pray for his strength when we are tempted to return to our former ways. Through prayer, reading the Bible, and godly counsel from mature believers, we need to daily seek his direction and guidance for our lives." This is the same message, but it is far more concrete and less likely to be misunderstood at this point in the believer's faith journey.

Metaphors

Metaphors are rhetorical devices that draw comparison between two things. Rather than a long or explicitly stated comparison, metaphors imply the similarity. They challenge listeners to transfer their associations with one concept to another: *Tad galloped down the path.* The word *gallop* fills the listener's mind with the image of a horse, and the speed associated with a horse's gallop. Metaphorical language requires the listener's mind to be more active and participative in reaching the meanings we want them to derive. The Bible contains many great metaphors that help our human minds transfer our thoughts and feelings about one thing onto that of another.

Jesus's thoughts toward the Pharisees are clear when he says to them in Matthew 23:33, "You snakes! You brood of vipers!" Calling them snakes and vipers is more powerful than simply saying they are being sneaky and potentially dangerous *like* snakes, or acting *as* vipers. Using the snake metaphor connotes a host of other common philosophies held toward snakes without having to list or spell them out.

Similarly, when he sees Jesus coming toward him, John says in John 1:29, "Look, the Lamb of God, who takes away the sin of the world!" The image of Jesus as a lamb—a common object of sacrificial offerings in that culture—is deeply meaningful in that context.

Later, in John 6:35, Jesus says, "I am the bread of life. Whoever comes to me will never go hungry, and whoever believes in me will never be thirsty."

The prophet Isaiah reminds himself (and us) of our proper relationship with the Lord when he declares, "We are the clay, you are the potter; we are all the work of your hand" (Isaiah 64:8).

Further, Jesus tells us we are salt and light in the world.

These metaphors all work with listeners as they transfer their understandings of snakes, lambs, bread, clay, salt, and light to form new understandings about the nature of God and those who serve him.

Two abstract concepts many of us confuse are sympathy and empathy. The use of abstract definitions to explain abstract concepts is often not enough. Using metaphor in a simple story, Dr. Les Parrott III, cofounder of the Center for Relationship Development at Seattle Pacific University, shared with me how he is able to easily explain for his students the difference between sympathy and empathy: "Here's the difference. Sympathy is standing on the shore and throwing a lifeline out to someone who is struggling in the water. Empathy is actually diving into the water, risking your own well-being, to bring them back to safety. It's heroic. And it's just as heroic when we do that in our relationships. Empathy is a rare experience."

Similes

As another type of figurative language, similes, like metaphors, serve as comparisons but, unlike metaphors, always use the words *like* or *as*. He ran *as fast as* a rabbit. If the listener has a mental image of the relative speed of rabbits, she immediately understands how fast the runner was.

I used a simile when I suggested that effective communication happens when our messages connect with listeners *like* burdock in a collie's fur. This simile only works, of course, if you've ever attempted to extract small, thorny plants tangled in a dog's fur. Similes help listeners transfer understanding from something they already know, to something new they don't yet know.

Jesus uses many similes, especially to explain what the kingdom of heaven is like. It is *like* a mustard seed (Matthew 13:31); *like* yeast (Matthew 13:33); *like* a hidden treasure (Matthew 13:44); *like* a man seeking pearls (Matthew 13:45); *like* a net cast into a lake (Matthew 13:47); *like* a homeowner who brings out new treasures as well as old from his storage room (Matthew 13:52); or *like* a landowner who set out to hire workers (Matthew 20:1). In most of those cases, Jesus also provides more details to explain the similes further so his meaning will be clear to all who listen. The similes Jesus uses are culturally relevant, and we can be assured that even the vague ones make more sense to Jesus's original listeners than they sometimes do to us without the help of some research.

Analogies

In the umbrella of figurative language, metaphors and similes are specific devices that can be used in single sentences to compare two things. Analogies, however, are usually more developed and complex, and they often embed metaphors and similes within themselves. An entire story may function as an analogy comparing two things with the intent of transferring understandings of the second thing to the first. Many of Jesus's parables include analogies. They offer vivid pictures to help hearers understand the nature of God (e.g., the prodigal son, Luke

15:11–32); or his nature as the sustainer and source of life (e.g., Jesus is the vine; we are the branches, John 15:5).

I once had a student deliver a self-introduction speech comparing himself to his car. Like his rusty, beat-up car, he too (he argued) wasn't much to look at, had been all over the nation, and was highly dependable. Transferring our understandings of older yet reliable cars, we could quickly form some images of the type of person this student was.

It's easy to be misled by overstated claims about tiny, nearly invisible hearing aids. Most of us don't really understand that specific technology, but we do understand how a small car can't pull a huge load. John Reiniche, owner of Hear for You in Manteno, Illinois, explains how he used this analogy to make a point very clear to his customer:

> Just last week I had this guy come into my office and ask about the "new, extended-wear, invisible-in-the-ear hearing aid" he saw in the paper. They are amazingly small and discreet devices. He asked me if they work.
>
> I told him, "Of course they do, for some people. But let me explain it this way. You have a hearing loss similar to a sixteen-foot trailer filled with three tons of firewood. You are asking me if you can pull that trailer with a Prius. The answer is no. You need a truck with a serious engine in it. These guys won't be right for you."

Outsourcing

Fortunately, there are myriad sources for us to draw from in the attempt to use similes, metaphors, and analogies to communicate spiritual concepts more effectively. The Bible remains the richest source, but among new believers or unbelievers, we can draw from contemporary life events to make connections. Stan Toler's book *The Inspirational Speaker's Resource: Tools for Reaching Your Audience Every Time*[1] is a great source not only for polished public speakers but also for any level of storied leader. A simple Google search using the keyword(s) of your topic, plus the word *analogies*, will likely reap some helpful (and some less than helpful) examples to sift through.

Many may not understand the theological concept of redemption. But everyone understands the concept of recycling. Adapting to his congregation, Dr. Ed Heck, the senior pastor of Kankakee First Church of the Nazarene in Illinois, uses the power of metaphor and analogy in this great identity story, providing a rich understanding of who Christ is as our Redeemer:

I read of an amazing orchestra in a poor village in Paraguay. The village is next to the landfill, and the people of the village make their living by picking through the 1,500 tons of trash that are dumped there every day. They pick through the trash with long hooks called *ganchos*, so the garbage pickers are called *gancheros*.

Favio Chavez, a young professional musician, saw the desperate poverty of the village and decided to start a small music school. Chavez lent out his small supply of five musical instruments but quickly had too many students. So Chavez asked one of the trash pickers, Nicholas Gomez, to make some instruments from recycled materials to keep the younger kids occupied. Gomez turned out to be a miracle worker: The instruments actually sounded good! The small school grew, and the students had a new sense of dignity, and the whole village came alive with hope.

Eventually, the students formed an orchestra of redeemed instruments—a cello made from an oil can; a flute from an old pipe; a drum set that uses X-rays as the skins; bottle caps that serve as the keys for a saxophone; a double bass from a large oil barrel; a violin from a salad bowl, and strings tuned with forks! They are called The Recycled Orchestra or, The Landfill Harmonic. You can Google them or hear them on YouTube.

Favio Chavez, the orchestra director, says, "The world sends us garbage. We send back music." Could there be a more powerful picture of the church of Jesus Christ? God rescues and redeems us from the garbage of brokenness and sin, and through the redemptive power of God's grace to us, by faith in Christ, we are redeemed and recycled, and we find our place with other redeemed people to form the church. We are able to make beautiful music together because of God's amazing grace. We become alive with dignity and hope.

Insourcing

Effective storytellers retell others' stories when they fit the teller's intended purpose (e.g., identity, vision, counter, challenge, or change). The best source of contemporary analogies, however, remains our own lives. These are *our* stories, *our* examples, *our* illustrations—so sharing them becomes more authentic for our listeners. And the best part is that exercising even some imagination opens our eyes to spiritual truths in the routine happenings of our everyday lives. The visible of our everyday lives offers insight into otherwise invisible spiritual truths. In Romans 1:20, Paul reminds us that "since the creation of the world God's invisible qualities—his eternal power and divine nature—have been clearly seen, being understood from what has been made, so that people are without excuse."

Bestselling author and speaker Stan Toler shared with me that he once landed in Jackson, Mississippi, for an engagement. He had been told to go to baggage claim and look for someone who would look like they were looking for him. "Unfortunately," Stan lamented, "no one seemed to be looking for me."

Using that story as an effective analogy later that same evening, he told his audience, "Let me take you to Acts 4:31–33, where you will discover a group of people who were looking for someone, and he was looking for them." The simple (and often humorous) happenings of our daily journeys provide rich analogies for theological truths if we simply learn to recognize them as such.

If you are a mother or father, you've undoubtedly seen the deepest of spiritual truths play out literally in front of you through your children: the battle of the selfish will, the fruits of the Spirit, unconditional love of the Father for his children, the painful consequences of poor decisions, and so on. Married? You've experienced spiritual truths of patience, love, submission, forgiveness, and speaking the truth in love. I seldom speak publicly without telling stories of my children, grandchildren, and wife (yes, the rabid Red Sox fan). My family is simply the petri dish in which abstract spiritual concepts have been most strongly tested and firmly grown within me.

Do you enjoy nature? Are you a nurse? Do you come from a dysfunctional family (who doesn't)? Do you have a blended family? Do you have pets? In short, your life—not mine or someone else's—can be your richest source of narrative illustrations. Knowing your listener or audience, which stories from your life will connect most effectively?

Heather Barkley, the director of communications at Huntington University in Indiana, shares this example of narratively connecting her life to illustrate a message on simplicity:

Periodically, I have opportunities to preach at our church. When I preached a message on simplicity, it was born out of reading the story of the rich young ruler as told in Luke 18:18–23. Never before had I interpreted this message as a call to simplicity until the Holy Spirit revealed that truth to me. Jesus is asking the rich young ruler to empty his life of the temporal to make room for the eternal.

Our congregation includes a significant number of folks for whom our church is their first experience with organized religion. Using my own concrete experience to unpack the abstract ideas of what is temporal and what is eternal was how I felt led to show the relevance of the passage to the current day. The rich young ruler's story prompted me to change my own priorities, and eventually led to my husband and me opening ourselves up to becoming foster parents. Sacrificing our selfishness has led to a joy-filled but challenging journey that made us overnight parents to three incredible children.

By sharing our story, in contrast to the rich young ruler's response, I hoped to encourage others to heed God's call for a simpler life—not for the sake of simplicity but to give God more room to work in our lives.

Communicating with Caution

Harnessing the power of narrative to communicate biblical truths makes sense. It was, after all, Jesus's primary form of communication.

As storied leaders, though, we need to use caution when using analogies, similes, and metaphors. We are not Jesus, and the potential problem with these narrative tools is that, like any other tool, they can be misused. We need to be careful that our analogies are true to biblical truths. The elaboration, for instance, of too many story elements can send unintentional messages. Dr. Kevin Zook warns that analogies "open windows for understanding while simultaneously sowing the seeds of misunderstanding."[2]

For example, even the parable of the prodigal son could possibly be misinterpreted if we (as the storytellers) aren't cautious to emphasize the intended message of the story. The son, after squandering his father's inheritance and living among the pigs, humbly returns. He is greeted by the open-armed, loving embrace of his father, who gives him a new robe, sandals, a ring, and a party. This is among our favorite analogies, comparing the unconditional love of this father for the undeserving son to God's own unconditional love for us. We can't help but see ourselves in this story, undeserving of God's love. Yet, Dr. Zook cautions us, a listener could possibly draw the additional conclusion that God not only forgives and loves us but also will always bestow material rewards upon us, which, of course, is not the intended message. Zook's point is valid; storied leaders share responsibility in the meaning-taking process. We must help guide the listener to the intended lessons from our analogies. We can do this most faithfully by offering a brief conclusion of the analogy's meaning.

Reflect or Discuss

1. In what ways do you think Christians' tendency to speak religionese creates confusion for new or nonbelievers?

2. Practice giving your own sixty-second testimony using only concrete language that could be understood by a twelve-year-old with little or no faith experience. It's harder than you'd think!

3. Which similes and metaphors have been most helpful for your understanding of who God is?

4. The author states that his family is the primary source from which he draws spiritual analogies. What are your primary sources? Why do analogies drawn from our own lives tend to be more effective?

5. Dr. Kevin Zook warns that analogies "open windows for understanding while simultaneously sowing the seeds of misunderstanding." Why do we need to be cautious when using analogies to communicate spiritual truths?

13   Speak to the Heart

Members squirm in their pews when pastors ask for special offerings to cover broken heating units, annual budget commitments, or simply to keep the lights on. *Why does the pastor always have to talk about money?* The answer is usually simple. Perhaps you have heard that many churches face the unfortunate paradox of being financially supported by only about 20 percent of the congregation, which includes the faithful giving of tithes and offerings. Can you imagine riding in a plane that was powered by only 20 percent of its engines?

When my own church needed to make an appeal for more giving, the treasurer prepared several PowerPoint spreadsheets of our income and expenses. There were a lot of numbers. I was asked to address the church family on behalf of our board. The numbers were real, important, and helped tell the story, but there were so many that they would have been mind-numbing for most. I reduced about eight budget slides to one. I kept the key numbers, showing the big picture of the income versus expenses equaling a deficit. The next two slides, however, were simply pictures of people. One was my son Tad (remember the kid who gave a hundred dollars?), and the other was my recently deceased mother-in-law, Shirley. After about one minute of talking through the numbers on the one slide, I advanced to the slide of my son. This is pretty much the rest of my message from that morning announcement:

Here's Tad. You'll notice two things about Tad here. One is the hundred-dollar bill he's waving in the air. It took Tad about seven months to earn this money. It came from allowances of three dollars a week. It came from birthday money from grandparents. It came from odd jobs inside and outside the house, lemonade stands, and creative capital ventures like selling original drawings from his lawn chair set up by the curb. It even came from Easter, after Tad told the Easter bunny at the mall that he only wanted cash, not candy, this Easter. Well, it all finally totaled up to one hundred, so this is a picture of him after the bank handed him this crisp bill. So that's the story behind the bill in his hand.

The other thing I want you to see is the smile on his face. Tad was so delighted to finally attain the bill he'd wanted for so long. And for what purpose? Video games? Candy? Stuffed animals? No. He told us he wanted it so he could give it to Jesus. The day after this photo was taken, Tad handed it to Mrs. Clupper in Sunday school.

This photo of a smiling woman is my mother-in-law, Shirley, whom many of you knew. In the last months of her life, her health made it impossible for her to attend our church. She was, however, fairly independent, still paying her few bills not covered by her assisted living center. Two weeks after she passed away, Jeanette received a phone call from Ray [who is the head usher at our church].

"Jeanette, this is Ray. I've got a check in my hand from your mother."

Having been ill, she had been unable to send off a tithe check in several weeks, so it was a fairly large check.

After a pause, he continued, "She must have sent it off shortly before she passed. I'm not sure what to do with it. I can certainly tear it up."

Jeanette's response was immediate. "Ray, you had better cash that check! Mom was a faithful tither all her life, and now even after her death. If you don't cash that, I'll have that woman haunting me!"

Our board wants you to know the numbers. They are real, and they are not currently adding up. Our church is committed to ministry, both local and abroad. This requires faithful giving. But more important than the numbers are the faces. We've seen the smiling faces of those served by ministry and missions, but this morning I wanted to show you the happiness that comes from giving—from the very young to the very old and all of us in between. You don't have to give 100 percent of your income, as Tad did. But it does require giving happily out of the abundant blessings of our hearts— giving back to him what is his.

The church needed to *know* something. The numbers represented the rational appeal for giving: *We can't pay our bills without it.* It was the case in black and white. But the church also needed to feel something— not guilt but, rather, the joy of giving as represented on the faces of two seemingly opposite people: a seven-year-old boy and an eighty-seven-year-old woman.

The Elephant and the Rider

Several years ago we took our kids to the circus. Their favorite part was during an intermission when parents drained their bank accounts to let their children climb atop a seven-ton elephant. Tad and Lucy, naturally, had to do this. As we made our way from our bleacher seats toward the elephant, one thing became clear: This thing was enormous. I questioned my judgment as a father when I watched my babies climb up the steel ladder, from which they stepped into seats on the elephant's back. Crazy-big beast! Now they were strapped in (along with several other children at the same time), but so what? Would mere straps provide protection from this perilously powerful pachyderm?

Granted, this particular pachyderm didn't seem perilous. The illustration is still poignant, however. Instead of children, imagine an adult trainer riding the elephant. If he weighs two hundred pounds, his size ratio is roughly 1/100 compared to the elephant. He might even carry a whip. But let's be real here. A 200-pound man (even carrying a whip!) will not be able to control a 20,000-pound elephant if the elephant develops other plans.

Chip and Dan Heath refer to this same image of riders on elephants—an analogy they attribute to University of Virginia psychologist Jonathan Haidt—to illustrate a powerful point about rationality and emotion in stories. The rider represents rationality, holding the reins and appearing to be in control. The elephant, however, represents our emotion. The rider's control is precarious because of the rider's relative size as compared to the elephant.[1] Similarly, God made us simultaneously rational and emotional. Like the rider, we want to be rational in our choice-making. Yet the power of emotion can often outmatch mere rationality. And it's a good thing, too. If we relied only on rationality, would any of us have a second child (or even more)? Give sacrificially to support missions for people we'll never meet? Forgive an enemy? Faithfully support a spouse through horrible sickness in addition to times of health? Submit the powerful will of self to the will of God? We rely on both rationality and emotion, but when push comes to shove, the elephant wins.

More than two thousand years ago, Aristotle taught the fundamentals of human persuasion (at least from a Western perspective). He argued that one could not be effective persuading an audience unless that person was first trusted. Therefore, speakers needed *ethos*, or, a reputation of credibility. Second, a speaker needed to appeal to logic—our sense of rationality. Without logic, we're left with groundless argument or, perhaps, mere emotional manipulation. So we need to utilize *logos*, or an appeal to rationality through facts. Lastly, Aristotle asserted that people are seldom moved from attitude to action unless they are emotionally motivated to do so. Charts, graphs, arguments, and lists of reasons are important for *logos*. But to inspire change, we need to engage listeners' hearts. *Pathos* appeals, therefore, are those that evoke emotional responses. And the primary way to make effective *pathos* appeals is—you guessed it—the story.

To be clear, emotional appeals and stories are not the only form of communication required for effective leadership. We wouldn't ever want to lead someone in a direction that is irrational. The facts cannot be ignored. Jesus urges us, in Luke 14:28, to make rational choices before deciding to carry the cross and follow him. "Suppose one of you wants to build a tower. Won't you first sit down and estimate the cost to see if you have enough money to complete it?" There is a cost to following Jesus; those who follow him need to *think* that through. They need to make an informed, reasoned choice before committing to a task that, to many, seems irrational—especially during the days when Jesus lived and walked on the earth.

Yet, just ten verses later, in the beginning of Luke 15, Jesus tells a story that also engages their hearts. He asks them to imagine themselves as shepherds leaving the ninety-nine and searching until finding the one lost sheep, which would bring them great joy and rejoicing. In the same way, he proclaims, there will be such rejoicing when one sinner repents.

Rationality remains in the driver's seat (e.g., count the cost), yet stories are still among the strongest tools to evoke appropriate emotions (e.g., joy and rejoicing). These emotions then motivate the body toward action (e.g., deciding that following Christ is worth the cost). They get the elephant moving.

□ □ □

What is hope? How would you describe it to someone? You might start with a dictionary definition. But how would you connect it to our minds and hearts? Corey MacPherson, the vice president of spiritual development and chaplain at Eastern Nazarene College, shared with me this example:

> I asked students to send me pictures of hope to use in a chapel message for the first week of Advent. One student's picture of hope was her brother, who has cerebral palsy: *This is a picture of my big brother, Brandon. He has cerebral palsy, so he is in a wheelchair and cannot talk. This is the perfect picture of hope, for he never ceases to be happy despite his disability.*
>
> Asking students for photos allowed them to participate in the message of our hope in Christ, and it reminded students that signs of hope are all around us, if we but pay attention.

As MacPherson's example illustrates, real stories of real people evoke *pathos*. Emotional understandings let us *feel*, in addition to merely knowing things. Some additional examples include:

- After providing a financial report to the congregation, the board secretary displays a photo of Julie. She's a little girl who recently accepted Christ through their children's church. He tells the story of how Julie's father was drawn to church by the softball ministry. Her mother then became active in the ladies' ministries. At a men's retreat, Julie's father accepted the Lord, and now Julie has done the same. He concludes by reminding everyone that giving isn't merely an obligation to make numbers balance on a budget. Giving is about seeing lives, like Julie's, transformed.

- Instead of merely lecturing about the dangers of alcohol to his son, a father becomes highly vulnerable and discloses how he once allowed alcohol to control his own life. He describes the heartache it caused for his parents and, ultimately, for himself. He explains how he initially sought alcohol as his escape but that, in time, it became a prison for him.

- A church has recently begun using social media. Rather than use it merely to announce programs, schedules, and mission statements, they use it to tell stories. They feature short testimonies (some written, some videotaped) from actual members telling what the Lord has done in their lives. These represent a broad cross section of the congregation, each with different circumstances but each containing the same story of redemption and changed lives. With the power of before-and-after selfies, these stories of real people touch hearts as well as minds with the hope of new life in Christ.

As Christian leaders, we want to communicate identity (*this is who we are*), vision (*this is where and who we can be*), counter stories (*this is actually the way things are*), and challenge (*with God's strength, you can make it*). Although we'll communicate these things in a variety of ways, one will include using stories. In addition to touching minds, stories are particularly effective at touching hearts for Christ. They engage emotions through the listeners' identification with real people and relationships. The more we can identify with the person in the story, the greater the emotional empathy. The greater the emotional empathy, the more we can apply the illustrated truths to our own lives.

Heart for the Homeless

One approximation of the annual number of homeless people in the United States is from a study by the National Law Center on Homelessness and Poverty, which estimates that between 2.3 and 3.5 million people experience homelessness in the United States.[2] The Substance Abuse and Mental Health Services Administration provides the following statistics about who is homeless:[3]

- 62% male
- 38% female
- 21.8% under age 18
- 23.5% ages 18 to 30
- 37% ages 31 to 50
- 14.9% ages 51 to 61
- 2.8% age 62 or older
- 41.6% white, non-Hispanic
- 9.7% white, Hispanic
- 37% black/African-American
- 4.5% other single races
- 7.2% multiple races

These constitute a lot of numbers, and they are a critical part of the full story of homelessness that needs to be told. It's difficult to imagine a few million homeless people, though. The breakdown of age, gender, and race is interesting, but it's not necessarily motivating. Further, these numbers aren't what Jesus cares about. Jesus cares about names and faces. Jesus cares about people. While we need the numbers as part of the *logos* appeal, we are less likely to be motivated to serve the homeless without a *pathos* appeal.

Author Joyce Williams, the Kansas field representative for MY HOPE with the Billy Graham Evangelistic Association, shared the following true story with me. She uses the metaphor of living water to communicate a deep theological truth. Further, notice how her story speaks directly to the heart, replacing numbers with names, faces, and stories. Which would motivate you to volunteer? More statistics, or Joyce's story?

Shimmering blisters of Kansas sun bubbled in the blinding heat of that July Saturday noon. With the temperature nudging toward a hundred degrees, it was a good day to be inside, in air-conditioned comfort, with a tall glass of iced tea. So what were almost thirty of us from eight to ten different churches doing on the sweltering pavement in downtown Wichita getting ready for a cookout? We were there because we knew that more than one hundred very special people—some of Wichita's homeless street people—would be coming for their luncheon appointment.

For several years, a number of churches have joined together in a united effort to feed the needy and homeless on Saturdays. The line of tables stretched in the shade of the swaying cottonwoods reminded me of Sunday dinners on the ground from my childhood. As the aroma of grilling burgers and hot dogs flung by fragrant fingers drifted along the city streets, people began to gather, calling greetings to one another. Old friends teased each other as they waited patiently in line. Before long, they moved through the line holding plates laden with burgers, hot dogs, potato salad, and even tossed salads splashed with ranch dressing. For whatever reason, we kept running out of hot dogs. As more came off the grill, it was worth another trip through the line to get one.

We were a melting pot of personalities and individuals. Jack was soon speaking fluent Spanish with several of our guests. A young Vietnamese man's face brightened when he was handed a full plate, even though he could not understand very much of what we said to him. Another man had just gotten out of jail. There was an older man who needed help when he walked.

With much practice and expertise, about thirty servers dispensed the food, along with cheery greetings and words of encouragement. We ranged from Betty, with her silvery curls circled by a headband, to six-year-old Ashley, her red hair glistening in the sun.

Little Ashley handed out bananas. A bunch of our friends took an extra one "for the road."

The scene was beautiful. There was no recrimination, no judgmental criticism, no sermonizing. From time to time, our friends quietly drifted toward Jack, Rick, or someone else and whispered about special needs. Pulling a tract or small Testament from a pocket, we were glad to point them to the answer. There were several vignettes featuring caring arms draped around lonely shoulders. Reverently in that outdoor cathedral, with branches swaying gently and grass growing underfoot, they softly prayed together. Everybody knew we cared. But the primary message taught that day was the one being lived out in flesh and blood.

Our friends couldn't get enough to drink. Huge jugs of water and lemonade quickly emptied. We kept refilling their big cups over and over. One lady handed her canteen to me to fill with lemonade. Unfortunately I was momentarily distracted, and I splashed some on the outside. She cried out in dismay, "You've ruined it! Now it will be sticky every time I touch it!" Realizing what a valuable item that container was to her, I painstakingly scrubbed the outside so it would be as good as new.

It was obvious to us on that sweltering day that life had handed a lot of lemons to these unfortunate friends. I was reminded of the words of Jesus encouraging us to give a cup of cold water in his name. As we dispensed jugs of lemonade and water, our hope was that they would see something in us that would give them hope. Maybe they could determine to take the lemons of life and mix them with the sweetness of the Lord. Then they, too, could taste the fresh and living elixir—the water of life—that lasts forever.

Later, as my new friend with the canteen was leaving, she turned to yell at me, "Hey, thanks for the lemonade—both inside and out!"

And I thought, *Yes! We want each of you to drink deeply of the sweet and living well that only peace with God can bring.* Although we had run out of lemonade on that hot day, the good news is that the living water that comes from God is an artesian well that springs up forever. It fills body and soul, inside and out, because its source is unlimited and everlasting.

Reflect or Discuss

1. While we are simultaneously rational and emotional beings, the author asserts that it is often emotion that ultimately moves us toward change. What are some decisions from your own life where something seemed irrational yet your heart told you it was right?

2. Leaving ninety-nine sheep to search for the lost one seems almost irrational. Yet what *emotions* drive the shepherd to save the lost sheep and, Jesus, lost souls?

3. Contrast the statistics on homelessness with the single story by Joyce Williams. Why would the story over the statistics be more likely to motivate one to help?

4. What are some current needs of your own church? In what ways could those needs be communicated through stories of real people and relationships?

5. When they are not careful, some speakers ignore reason and rationality altogether, resulting in something that feels like emotional manipulation. How can we be cautious to avoid this?

6. How are you and your church telling stories that evoke the emotions all seek on their journeys: hope, love, peace, contentment, and joy?

14   Keep It Real

Thanks to social media, I now know so much more about you. I know that you are always smiling and have good hair. Your spouse and children are always well-dressed and beautiful. They always do and say the funniest things. Even your pets are adorable. You always eat gourmet meals (thanks for sharing the photos!), take awesome vacations, and have the most faithful workout routines. I'm also humbled by your devotional life and the frequent, inspirational scriptures you post. And if you follow me on social media, you see the same. Different faces, pets, vacation spots, and witty stories, but the same theme: a perfect life!

Don't get me wrong; I feel very blessed in my life. And my pets are truly hilarious. I, however, am not perfect. I don't always smile. I'm not always funny; sometimes I'm just tired, cranky, and can snap at my family. I only dress nicely when I must. Frequently I wear mismatched socks. I eat tuna out of a can. I obsessively pick my nails. I skip a lot of workouts. This is the real me.

My social media self isn't a lie; it's just the carefully constructed version I put in the window for any passersby to see. Sociologist Erving Goffman referred in the 1950s to this careful presentation of ourselves as a daily process of "impression management."[1] Or, in the words of William Shakespeare, "All the world's a stage, and all the men and women merely players."[2] While social media may be the biggest stage available, we all live on various stages regardless. Hopefully you don't leave the house without making sure you've combed your hair, brushed your teeth, and pulled on pants, but when you enter the stage of life, how real are you?

As leaders, we have the most potential to influence others when we keep it real. Obviously, there are extremes that are entirely inappropriate—the guy who documents his wart surgery online, or the woman who lets you know of her four failed marriages within five minutes of meeting her. Or if I very publicly share a testimony that shifts from God's transforming power to a highly personal and detailed confession of my sins, it becomes more about me than about God, and has you wishing you could hit the mute button. Being real isn't about airing our dirty laundry.

Yet leaders need to be real. Who wants to take parenting advice from the guy who has you believing that he and his children have always been perfect and parenting is a breeze? Who can be encouraged in their faith by the woman whose faith has never been rocked by temptation, heartache, a major challenge, or serious doubt? Sharing airbrushed stories does more harm than good. They're not true. This approach sends all sorts of unhealthy and mixed messages about faith. It may imply a prosperity gospel (the idea that perfect faith in God results in a perfect and materially prosperous life). Major dissonance then occurs when one's new faith does not usher in prosperity. Her ex-husband still avoids paying child support, the physical diagnosis remains serious, and alcohol still threatens to end his sobriety.

The basic logical enthymeme we discussed in chapter 11 explains how change stories work. Stories function as enthymemes from which listeners draw conclusions: *Since that happened to her and since I am like her, it can happen to me too.* That's great if the story is one of truth. But when it's not, we are leading listeners toward falsehood. When my faith stories suggest or imply perfection, they are not true. They might still inspire change in the listener, but this new belief will be rocked with dissonance when it is found to be untrue. Faith is *not* fantasy. Jesus is not Santa Claus.

Scars without Scares

We lead best when we are honest. From places of pain come promise and peace. James boldly challenges us to "consider it pure joy, my brothers and sisters, whenever you face trials of many kinds, because you know that the testing of your faith produces perseverance. Let perseverance finish its work so that you may be mature and complete, not lacking anything" (James 1:2–4). As a leader, you may be currently experiencing this type of maturity and completeness. But don't forget where it (and you) came from. The ones you lead may already be amidst trials of many kinds, and if not, soon shall be. What they need are our real stories of Christ's faithfulness amidst our own trials. Scars represent healing. We can acknowledge our scars as evidence of Christ's transformative power. And we can do this without rolling up our pant legs and lifting our shirts to frighten others with every lurid detail that led to them. As a perfect example of keeping it real, check out excerpts from a sermon that the chaplain of Olivet Nazarene University, Mark Holcomb, shares with us here:

My fifth- to seventh-grade years were possibly the worst and darkest years of my life. We moved from a small town in southern Michigan to the big city, Grand Rapids. In the process, I lost friends, my baseball team, and a home I had grown to love. In Grand Rapids I had none of these. As the new kid on the block, I was the one chosen over a period of time to be the butt of every joke. Every other kid in my elementary school was relieved that it was me and not them.

I went through a time where I wouldn't be chosen for a pick-up game on the playground, I would get cut from every team I tried out for, or if the team I was on didn't cut me, I learned what it meant for the first time in my life to sit the bench.

Following these two years, we moved, and I changed schools, and just when I thought things were changing for the better, I was molested by a babysitter.

I don't think I could have been at a lower point in my life. Those years are lost, never to be given back. I felt abandoned, friendless, and betrayed. My sense of security was taken from me. I will never understand why these things happened to me, and I asked that question often, never receiving an adequate answer. I'm not a believer that there is a devil around every bush or corner waiting to pounce on us, but I do believe that the enemy will use anyone or anything; he'll use whatever he can to destroy any or all of us. He has us all in his crosshairs.

But I found myself asking questions like: *Is this my life? Is this how I am going to be defined? Are these the events that will shape who I am and who I will be?*

The answer was yes. This was and is my life. I was and am shaped by these events. I don't tell you any of these things to make you feel sorry for me but to let you know that in all this, I discovered something about myself and about God. I realize now, looking back through the rearview mirror, that in those moments when I couldn't rescue myself, when my life seemed to be shrouded in despair, God was with me and I wasn't alone.

Those words aren't spoken flippantly. My pain, although a long time ago, was real. But God's presence is the only explanation for why my life didn't totally unravel. My parents were aware of what was going on at my school, but I couldn't muster up the courage to tell them about the other incident until I was in my thirties, after carrying the shame for twenty years.

I don't want the message of what I'm trying to say to get lost in my story. We all have a story. I do want you to know that, by the grace of God, I'm not haunted by these things. I don't forget them, but I am free from them. I tell you this about myself to help you understand the hows and whys God has been able to restore for me, to redeem my story. And the reason God can restore and redeem us in the middle of all our junk is that, to answer Joan Osborne's question, God *was* one of us.

We are often more effective in storytelling when we keep it real. Projecting perfection would be robbing God's glory anyway, wouldn't it? After all, his strength is made perfect in our weakness (2 Corinthians 12:9). While there are times we tell others' stories, historical stories, or contemporary news stories, often the most powerful story we can tell is our own. A story is given more weight when we say, "This happened to me." Effective communicators often draw examples and illustrations from their own experiences (professions, childhood, marriage, children/grandchildren, pets, or hobbies). Our everyday experiences provide powerful spiritual lessons and illustrations. Rather than pretend to be perfect or people they are not, good storytellers keep it real. Their best stories are about themselves—often self-deprecating and sometimes vulnerable. Their transparency builds credibility and identification with an audience. Additional examples include:

- When inviting someone to your church, don't merely list programs and times. Rather, explain the role and impact this church has had in your life and for your whole family. Then offer a few specific examples of programs your children are highly involved in and/or things you personally appreciate about the worship services and pastoral staff.

- Speaking at a retreat, Janet uses several illustrations from having raised four boys. These stories have the audience laughing, wincing, and crying, but they are also powerful illustrations of biblical truths because they are real and have been experienced firsthand by a mother with whom her audience can identify.

- In a recent service, our pastor anointed a woman who has been suffering from depression since the death of her daughter several years ago. When the prayer time ended, she and her husband began to make their way back to their seats. Just then a teenage girl stood. In front of all, she spoke through tears to proclaim the Lord's faithfulness in her experiences with depression. Her obedience to be real with her own story (and again, leave out unnecessary details) was the testimony of encouragement that drew us all closer to Christ.

- As a new neurosurgeon in town, Mary started attending church. She was invited to a small gathering of ladies for lunch. Although some were initially intimidated by her degrees and her profession, that didn't last long. She had everyone laughing with her self-deprecating stories that revealed she was far from perfect and faced the same challenges as a wife and mom that the other ladies did.

Striking a Chord

I dare you. Go ahead and ask either my wife or me who the most optimistic person is on the planet. We'll both shout the same answer: *Dennis Crocker!* Of Dennis, I often say this: Had he perished on the Titanic, he would have told St. Peter, "It was really a lovely cruise, and that iceberg was such a majestic creation of God!" Lest you start to think his optimism and positivity come from having lived a life free of heartache, trust me, that isn't the case. He and his wife, Jeannie, have faced heartache, but they have clung to the Lord. Dennis, the vice president for Academic Affairs at Olivet Nazarene University, keeps it very real. Here he provides insight into how he uses his musical background and personal transparency to keep it real as a storied leader:

Basically, a conductor imposes his or her will on the ensemble; there's just really no way to get around that. So, for me, it has seemed important to identify and reinforce those moments in a rehearsal or performance when I can connect with the folks in the ensemble on an emotional level. I want them to know me as a person—someone who has a family, kids, a mortgage, etc.—and not just an arrogant, tyrannical despot bent on world domination through music!

I've used stories from my family and my kids to help me connect with my students and ensemble members. I have been willing to be somewhat transparent to help them get to know me. At an appropriate level, I have wanted my ensemble members to see some of my struggles and challenges, to know that I'm a real person, like them.

Many of the most profoundly meaningful experiences in my life have been connected to music. This story is no exception.

In the 1990s, I attended a choral music reading session in Kansas City. The composer, Craig Courtney, was present to represent his music and publisher. He introduced a new choral composition based on texts from Isaiah 43, "Be Not Afraid," and he set it for SATB [soprano, alto, tenor, and bass] voices and descant.

Be not afraid, for I have redeemed you; Be not afraid, I have called you by name.

When you pass through the waters I will be with you;
When you pass through the floods, they will not sweep o'er you;
When you pass through the fire you will not be consumed;
You are mine, you are precious in my sight.

Craig told us that within a year the community of Sioux City, Iowa, and the church itself were flooded. They had no idea how important and personal the words from the prophet would be to them.

Craig went on to tell the 150 conductors present about the deeply personal meaning the piece held anew for him and his own family after the sudden and unexpected death of his own son. He told us that he had no idea he was really composing the piece for himself.

I, too, have a personal connection with the piece, and I've shared this story over the years with several choirs and groups. I directed music at Kansas City First Church of the Nazarene for a few years. During that time, we felt that our ministry there should draw to a close. My wife, Jeannie, was pregnant, and with the complications she was experiencing, we felt that it was best for us not to have the additional stress of the church assignment.

Shortly after I resigned, Jeannie's pregnancy became critical. We lost the baby at six months and came very close to losing Jeannie too. Those were very, very dark days in our family. During those days we leaned heavily on those words from Isaiah. The words Craig Courtney paraphrased described our family's journey. We sensed God's buoyant, sustaining grace underneath and supporting us. God can be trusted completely, and he does answer prayer, but not always as we might anticipate or request.

I was able to share this story with my college choir when I was teaching and preparing to perform the piece. I told them that I wished I could guarantee that if they served the Lord, they and their families would be spared from suffering and pain. As we learned the piece and later performed it, I could see on their faces and hear in their voices the confirmation that I had been able to connect with my students in communicating the meaning and emotion in the words and music.

In looking back at more than twenty years of work with college and university choirs, I think this is probably one of the more effective opportunities I've had to keep it real.

What's your story? As a storied leader, the transforming power of Christ in you is your best story. Tell it. And keep it real.

Reflect or Discuss

1. In what ways (and from whom) do you feel pressure to present yourself as closer to perfect than you are?

2. How can our image of having it all together actually hurt others in their faith development?

3. The author suggests we need to show our scars without frightening listeners with gory details. Explain how we do that. How did Chaplain Mark Holcomb's story demonstrate that?

4. If we're not careful, talking about our pasts can inadvertently glorify or draw undue attention to the sin we have left behind. How can we avoid this error while still telling our before-and-after stories to inspire change and glorify Christ?

5. To what extent do you keep it real? Who in your life could be encouraged in their faith journey if you could be more authentic about your own journey?

15 Play Small Ball

As baseball contemporaries just after the turn of the twentieth century, Ty Cobb and Babe Ruth both ruled the game and set long-standing records. Although both are considered great, they had distinctively different styles of play. Ruth was a slugger, hitting 714 home runs, while Cobb only hit 117 in roughly the same number of years in uniform. That's six times as many! Cobb, however, had 4,191 hits compared to Ruth's 2,873. Cobb also had a career batting average of .367, a record that has yet to be beaten. These statistics almost sound contradictory. Ruth hit so many more home runs than Cobb, yet Cobb had so many more hits and a higher batting average. The difference, of course, is *how* they hit. Ruth swung for the fences. Cobb swung to get on base. Both styles can win games. Ruth's style resulted in record numbers of strikes. Cobb's style has been sometimes referred to as small ball.

Rather than swing for the low-percentage home run, Cobb swung to get on base. This resulted in many RBIs (runs batted in) and a record number of stolen bases that led to runs scored. He set long-standing records for both hits and runs scored. As mastered by Cobb, small ball is about getting on base; scoring is made possible by the efforts of those following in the lineup. It's a higher-percentage means of getting the ball in play than merely swinging for the home run. It also places faith in those who follow you in the lineup. Baseball is, after all—perhaps more than any other sport—a team effort.

Getting On Base

We need to keep our goals for storytelling in perspective. As with The Babe, there are some speakers with the rhetorical skill to hit home runs, igniting the minds and hearts of listeners to points of decision. For most of us, however, this is not necessarily a high-percentage approach. The father frustrated with his teenager may rack his brain for a story that will inspire radical change. Visiting a discouraged friend, you might wish you had a challenge story that would fully restore all hope and relieve anxiety. Sitting beside an unchurched parent at the soccer game, you want to construct an identity story that will portray every wonderful part of your church.

Instead, we should just try to get on base. As storied leaders, we need to realize that stories are neither magical spells nor antidotes. Over other forms of communication, narrative has great power to influence minds and engage hearts. But stories are still just one form of communication and are sprinkled within the full context of conversation. And effective communication depends as much on the listener as it does on the speaker. The listener may not be fully open to your message, regardless of how well you craft it. Depending on the listener's present position, baby steps may signal enormous progress.

Choose a Focus

When we attempt to accomplish too many goals with a single story, sermon, or lecture, we run the risk of accomplishing none of them. Listeners can become lost in too many details, plot twists, or lessons attempting to be taught. In contrast, effective communicators often have a primary message they hope a listener will grasp from a story, knowing there will be another time to expand or build upon that foundation. For example:

- Your son is furious with his friend. The friend has apologized, but your son feels the friend doesn't deserve forgiveness. Seeing an opportunity to teach him about God's grace, you wait until he is calm. You tell him a brief story from your own life when you were wronged and realized you needed to show grace to someone who had not earned it, much as Christ has done for us. You chose that particular story with the one goal of illustrating grace. You didn't expand it or combine it with others to reinforce values of friendship, honesty, or the controlling of our anger.

- A speaker at a teenage girls' retreat is torn. She realizes there are many challenges facing girls today that could be addressed. Ultimately, she chooses to focus on finding one's self-worth in Christ, and chooses a story or two to help illustrate this truth. She realizes that if she searches for a story or combination of several stories to communicate multiple truths, the girls might have a hard time discerning what the message is, and the speaker will ultimately have less impact on them.

- In the middle of a church board discussion about whether to cut some money from the budget by eliminating the coffee and doughnut social time between services, Harold offers a quick story about his conversation with Brandon. Brandon is someone new to the church, and he loves this social time because it enables him to meet people. Having the drink and food in his hands somehow just makes him feel more relaxed as he mingles. Harold's story does not attempt to solve the budget problem, propose alternative options, or condemn those who want to eliminate it. It does, however, challenge the board to think about what might be lost with hasty cuts.

Lauren Seaman is an urban missionary, called to the city of Chicago as part of an exciting ministry called Reach77. Lauren encounters people who represent a wide range of beliefs. Rather than swing for the fences, Lauren realizes the power of small ball, in connecting Christian truths to a person's particular faith narrative. Consider this example Lauren shares:

> One of the more difficult concepts for a Muslim to embrace is the belief in a triune God. (As a Christian, I humbly submit that it remains a mystery to me as well!) But for Muslims, Allah is so holy, so other, that there is no room for complexity beyond one. Allah cannot share authority or reverence.

Similarly, Christians believe in one God, though uniquely expressed in three persons: Father, Son, and Holy Spirit. As such, my Muslim friends mistakenly label Christians as polytheistic, while Christians clearly maintain their monotheism.

While I was visiting with friends in a country in North Africa, this contentious theological conundrum was raised. "Allah is one," they professed. "Allah cannot be three." In that moment, I wasn't sure I could convince them that Allah exists in three persons. However, I wondered, could I convince them Allah exists in two forms? If I could cause them to move from one to two, we were making progress.

So I posited: "Do you believe Allah is present here? Now?"

Their reply: "Yes!"

"Do you believe Allah is where my wife is right now, across the Atlantic?"

Hesitantly, "Yes…"

I followed with, "Is it possible for you to be here and there simultaneously?"

"Of course not," they retorted. I asked why. "Because," they said, "we only exist as one being, we are only able to be here or there, not in both places at once."

"But," I asserted, "you admit that Allah can be in both places at once. How can Allah be in both places at once?"

"By his spirit."

"You believe Allah can be expressed in spirit form?"

"Yes…"

"So Allah is one, but Allah is also spirit?"

"Hmmm…"

"Christians believe this too!" I exclaimed. I went on to explain that Christians believe in the expression of God as Holy Spirit, and that we also believe God can be in both places at once.

Admittedly, my friends did not profess faith in Jesus Christ that night. What this conversation did, however, was open up the possibility in their minds that God *could* exist hyper-dimensionally. If they could believe in *two* expressions of Allah, who is *one*, could they believe in a third...? I decided to leave that up to the Holy Spirit.

Perfect Vision

How's your vision? No, I don't mean your optical prescription. How are your priorities and your ability to identify and focus on what is most important? I know I can get distracted by a lot of small stuff that, ultimately, is not that important. What if you wanted to communicate that very specific message about vision to someone? When Dr. Kent Olney, chairman of Behavioral Sciences and professor of sociology at Olivet Nazarene University, needs to illustrate vision, he tells this real story about John:

I grew up with deaf siblings and have used sign language my entire life. So no one was surprised when, after seminary, I accepted a position as the pastor of a deaf congregation. One of the first deaf men I met in my new congregation was John. Four years older than me, John had a brilliant mind, a winsome personality, and a twinkle in his eyes that punctuated every interaction.

However, John also had juvenile diabetes that slowly began to destroy his body. First, his sight began to fail. After multiple eye surgeries, John's days of traveling and photography—two hobbies he enjoyed and that we often discussed together—came to a screeching halt. His eyes had been his pathway for communication, his gateway to the world. Now he could barely see. Communication became challenging, now that visits required adjusting the light so John could read my signs out of the corner of his one usable eye.

Not long thereafter, John's kidneys shut down. Hours at the dialysis center began to occupy his weeks.

Then came that fateful day at the large university hospital when John received news that his left leg needed to be amputated. I was in the room with him when the doctor explained that uncontrolled infections were ravaging the leg and threatening his life. Months later, John surrendered his right leg to amputation as well. Both amputations occurred just below the trunk.

John could not hear. He lost all but a flicker of sight in the corner of one eye. He lost the use of his kidneys. He lost both his legs. It was as if his body were being eaten away piece by piece.

Remarkably, John maintained a joy and buoyancy that amazed everyone who knew him. As a young man, he had committed his life to Jesus Christ. Since his life was no longer his own, he refused to surrender to despair. John believed that God was sovereign, even over the big disappointments of life.

I noticed our conversations begin to change. Instead of talking about travel and photography, two new themes became dominant. John consistently inquired about his friends and about heaven. A visit with John inevitably unfolded with questions like these: "How's Jenny doing? Did Bill raise that money he needed for his project? Is Peter feeling better? What do you think heaven will be like? Will we know each other there? Do you think people in heaven ever want to return to earth? What will our new bodies be like?"

I could count on it: Friends and heaven occupied John's thoughts and filled hours of conversation between us.

When John died in 1996, at the age of forty-four, I realized that his vision was actually far superior to mine. I watched his deteriorating body for more than a decade, counted his multiplied losses, and observed his tragedies. John's vision, on the other hand, allowed him to see what really mattered—relationships and eternity.

I have been challenged to adjust my vision ever since those days with John.

You probably recognize Dr. Olney's story as a perfect example of a challenge story in its form. It illustrates adaptation (chapter 12) with the use of optical vision as a metaphor for identifying spiritual priorities. It also demonstrates the principle of speaking to the heart (chapter 14); listeners quickly develop an emotional identification with and for John. In addition, it represents the concept of small ball because Dr. Olney uses the story to communicate one clear theme: vision.

Leadership is multifaceted. We lead by modeling. We lead by our actions. We lead by what we say and also by what we don't say. Storied leadership is but one aspect of how we can engage others on their faith journeys. In an hour-long conversation with a hurting friend, one story designed to reach a desired goal (e.g., identity, vision, counter, challenge, or change) might consume less than a minute. It's merely part, not the whole, of a conversation.

Choose a story with a focused goal. Tell it well. A home run would be great, but the important thing is to get on base. Success does not rely completely on you. There are no MVP awards in evangelism; do what you are called to do and trust that others will be called to the plate behind you. What Christ has done for you, he will do in the lives of others. We can be part of their journeys, but he who began a good work in *them* will be faithful to complete it (paraphrased from Philippians 1:6).

Reflect or Discuss

1. To what extent do you think your sense of responsibility and drive for achievement make you feel pressure to hit home runs of influence rather than merely getting on base? How is this home-run mindset not scriptural?

2. The author urges us to choose a focus for our stories rather than try to accomplish too many goals with them (or blitz the person with too many stories). How can we know which is the most important focus in any given setting?

3. What does the author mean by there being no MVPs in evangelism? How do we sometimes approach evangelism as if there *were* MVP awards?

4. Dr. Olney's story about John has the single focus of communicating vision to his listeners. It, likewise, is an outstanding example of speaking to the heart (chapter 13). Explain.

16 Capitalize on Context

The Bullhorn Speech

I was in my office when Jeff ran in one morning to tell me that one of the towers of the World Trade Center in New York had been hit by a plane. We gathered by a classroom television to watch in horror as the events unfolded.

That was September 11, 2001. I'm sure you remember where you were too. I'll bet you also remember a three-minute event that occurred just three days later, on the fourteenth of September. President George W. Bush stood atop the smoking rubble at Ground Zero, his arm around a firefighter. Speaking through a bullhorn, Bush delivered one of the best speeches of his life.

As president of the United States, Bush could have delivered that speech from anywhere, including the Oval Office. The choice to speak in that context—atop the rubble—was strategic and highly effective. Sometimes as important as *what* we say, is *where* and *when* we say it. The context of a message conveys great meaning. For our president, the location signaled his immediate presence (as opposed to distant) at the very heart of our focus. He then stood waving the small U.S. flag after his remarks, which sparked unifying national pride for viewers. The scene itself sent clear messages: *We will not cower and hide. The*

American spirit of freedom will not be deterred by evil. His speech likely would have still been effective if he gave it elsewhere—after all, American emotions ran very high for several days, weeks, months after 9/11—but would it have been so memorable? Most of us have forgotten the words he spoke, but we remember the image of him standing there. We remember the way it made us *feel.*

Places and Spaces

A story's impact is affected by where and when it is told. Different places and spaces evoke sensory information we attach as part of the message delivered at that place, at that specific time. A story told precisely when someone needs to hear it is so much more powerful than when that person's attention is elsewhere. The context of where and when a story is told magnifies its meaning, becoming part of the story itself. Try telling spooky ghost stories around a campfire under the noonday sun. You'll find the stories are the same—minus the scary.

The reason context impacts a story is rooted in emotion. Most things in our everyday lives are emotionally neutral. However, when we encounter them in an emotional situation or context, they may become associated in our minds with those corresponding emotions.[1] An intense emotion aroused by an event may lodge that event in our memory.[2] It's what makes it stick with us. Researchers refer to this association as crossover memory.[3] Our memories are affected by the emotions we experience at the time we encounter an event.

A particular situation or context can evoke emotion. That emotion magnifies and becomes associated with the event taking place there. Our recollections about that event are triggered and aided by our emotions—or, how we felt. It becomes easier to remember stories and messages triggered by emotion. The emotional imagery of our president standing firm atop the rubble triggers our memories. Though we may not recall every detail of his speech, we remember the patriotic pride we felt.

Further, the novelty or unusual nature of a situation draws our attention and affects our retention. A few years ago, our church ran a vacation Bible school that featured several consecutive evenings of great lessons, games, and activities. I'm fairly certain, however, which evening the children who attended will remember most vividly. Our church was swept with darkness as the power went off amidst tornado sirens. Nearly a hundred children sat lined up against basement hallways as teachers holding flashlights led them in our Bible school songs.

My point is not that storytellers have to sensationalize their stories in order to evoke dramatic emotions. We don't have to turn the lights out on an audience to affect their attention to or retention of our message. In fact, using gimmicks to sensationalize a message may backfire—with the person or audience only remembering the gimmick, not the message behind it. Rather, we should be aware that the context of when and where we tell a story do become part of the story that is told. Our goal, then, is to be mindful of our context. What context would be most congruent with our message? What context could set the appropriate tone or atmosphere for our message? What setting (place, space, or timing) will most effectively reinforce our story for retention of its core message?

For the past several years, I've taken one of my leadership classes on a field trip. Our bus stops at a local auto dealership. I ask them to look around and make observations about how cars are displayed. Eyes widen as our bus then ventures to our next location at the end of a gravel road—a junkyard. We exit the bus and walk two hundred yards through the surreal automotive graveyard. Smashed windshields. Horribly mangled doors. Imaginations suggest stories of tragedy. Finally we stop, surrounded by the hundreds of twisted, rusting cars. They, and we, are far from the public's eye.

I ask them to compare what they observed at the dealership to what they observe here. New cars glistened, were parked to attract attention, and looked flawless. In contrast, these are hidden from view, broken, and they all suggest stories. Standing in a small circle there, I draw the comparison to the people we are called to serve. On the outside, many people look like new cars. On the inside, however, many feel like these junkyard cars that surround us. Each has a story. Many feel broken, pushed aside, rejected. This activity always sparks a dialogue about our roles as servant leaders.

We could hold that same discussion from our air-conditioned classroom, but I don't think the message would be experienced in the same way. They would understand but won't have *experienced*, seen, even smelled, it. They would not *feel* the message. The context helps shape not only the meaning of the message but also our long-term memory of the message.

□ □ □

When our son T.J. was in high school, he called one afternoon from the school, an emotional wreck. His relatively new iPod had been stolen from his P.E. locker. It had cost so much, and he had no means by which to replace it. He was so distraught that I picked him up from school. As I drove, he vented a range of emotions—the primary one being anger. He was livid. Although he couldn't prove it, he was just sure he knew the boy who had done it. That boy had a reputation. He had stolen before. *How he hated him!* T.J. shook as he talked. I listened and drove.

There we were in this odd place and time. I should have been at work; he should have been at school. Instead, I found myself alone with my distraught son. But he was also a captive audience. I asked him more about the boy he was so sure had stolen the iPod. What was his story? What was he like? What would lead the boy to steal? Did he have a father to whom he could vent his problems? As we drove, we talked about grace. We talked about the value of that boy, who likely had far worse pain in his life than losing an iPod. To T.J.'s surprise, I pulled the car up to a store. I took him inside and bought him a new iPod. I explained that, while I wasn't obligated to give him this gift, I was choosing to do so freely, which is a lot like what grace looks like. My message—the story of grace—could have been told anywhere, but because of the context in which we found ourselves, I found a listening and receptive heart. Since his emotions of anger and injustice were at such a heightened state, the timing was right for him to associate—and transfer—them into emotions of forgiveness and unwarranted favor. Further, my intent was not merely to give T.J. a new iPod, but—hopefully—a new story.

The hero he needed was not a father with a gift but, rather, a heavenly Father with grace. Isn't that the story we all seek?

Remember the Monomyth? People not only see and describe their lives as one large journey; they also see their daily lives as a series of smaller journeys. On our journeys, we face struggles and conflicts while we search for resolution. It's the fundamental narrative pattern. Some struggles are as trivial as a broken microwave, spilled milk, or even a stolen iPod. Others are far greater: cancer, job loss, loneliness, accepting one's own mortality, and so on. It's when we face these larger struggles that we find ourselves searching for a hero—someone or something that will fix the brokenness, bringing freedom and peace. When we encounter another person who is at this point, the context is right. It's the right time to enter one's story and lead. Do they need to understand an identity (of you, themselves, Christ, or your church), a vision for what could be, a counter to an anti-story, a challenge, or motivation to change?

Planning Places

Sometimes a situation spontaneously presents itself such that the time and place are obvious—right here, right now. For other times, however, we can plan our spaces and places for storied leadership. The junkyard experience, for example, is highly planned. The challenge for leaders is to think through what the message is as well as the best context in which to deliver it. Should it be delivered face to face, over coffee? Out of the office? Over the phone? At a particular place that holds meaning for one or both of you? In the presence of someone important to the other? The environment communicates a message and evokes emotions. Which environment would reinforce the power of your message? Which place would make the message more memorable?

Some examples:

- As co-leader of a young men's accountability group, I wanted to emphasize the principle of dying to self, so we took the men to a local graveyard, at night. There in the darkness, we stood in a circle reading by flashlight scriptural references to the dying of self. The setting had an enormous impact on the message. We spoke solemnly, just above a whisper. Following a brief discussion of our need to replace our own strong wills with the will of the Father, we dispersed. The context intensified the message and made it memorable.

- A father takes his thirteen-year-old daughter to an upscale restaurant, where he presents her with a purity ring. As he shares the story of God's desire for our sexual purity, he explains that the ring can represent her commitment to abstinence before marriage. The timing is important (delivering it to her at age thirteen, not at age five, or twenty-one). Likewise, the atmosphere communicates the significance of the message—one she will always remember.

- Your son has just had his heart broken by a girl. Being careful not to minimize his experience, you take him for a walk and share with him your own experience of heartache when you were about that same age, and of God's faithfulness throughout. For a moment in time, you two seem to have everything in common. Hearing that story prior to his breakup (the timing) might have had little impact, and hearing it later on the couch while watching television (the location) would have had far less impact than away from distractions on the walk. The context helped shape the meaning.

- Fundraising and financial pledges are coming in slower than necessary to complete the church addition of a new family life center. Toward the end of the service, the pastor asks everyone to get up and follow him. They walk outside and onto the poured concrete slab that holds the skeleton of steel studs, beams, and trusses. He asks everyone to remember their vision for how lives will be changed in this place, but before that change can happen, everyone must be faithful with their pledges. While he could say the same words from the pulpit, speaking from this context intensifies the message dramatically for all who stand there, reminded that completion of their vision requires their faithfulness to their commitments.

Reflect or Discuss

1. Do you remember the feeling you got from former President George W. Bush's bullhorn speech after 9/11? How did the context of that message impact its meaning for us?

2. How do the spaces, places, and timing of our stories contribute to emotional associations, thus making them memorable for listeners?

3. Recall a story that you remember in part due to the context in which it was shared with you. What aspects of that context led to its impact?

4. Whom do you know who needs encouragement in some aspect of his or her faith journey? How could your message be more meaningful for him or her with a careful choice of context?

5. What message does your church want to communicate internally (to the congregation itself) or externally (to the community)? How could these messages have greater impact if delivered in different contexts?

17   Break Expectations

The ball game ended just before ten o'clock p.m. At the age of twenty-two, my buddy Chris and I were still somehow hungry after eating our way through all nine innings. After only fifteen minutes on the interstate toward home, we took an exit to grab a bite. There in East St. Louis, we searched for something still open. Finally, a Dairy Queen!

Treats in hand, we sat outside the store at a white table with a canopy umbrella. A few spoonfuls into my Blizzard, I heard the sound of firecrackers behind me. Then Chris, wide-eyed as he faced the sound, dove to the ground. They weren't firecrackers; they were gunshots. I turned to see a man standing thirty feet from us. He stood next to the open door of his car and held out a gun, piercing the quiet darkness with loud bursts of fire. Chris got to his feet, sprinted inside the Dairy Queen, and flipped the inside lock on the glass door. Only the shooter and I remained. I sprang to the ground, my heart pounding against the asphalt parking lot, and lay, cringing, to wait for what would come next.

One way to capture and hold the attention of a listener or audience is to create suspense by utilizing the unexpected. Several years ago, legendary radio host Paul Harvey had a segment called The Rest of the Story, in which he would tell a story that always led up to a sudden twist or unexpected ending followed by his iconic final sentence, "And now you know...the *rest* of the story." Good storytellers often create and sustain listener interest through some form of suspense. Once our interest is piqued, our attention is fixed until we hear how the story ends.

What did you do?

What choice did she make?

Was he all right?

So what happened?

Another way to utilize the power of the unexpected is to catch a listener or audience off guard with something shocking that breaks their expectations until the rest of your story clarifies your meaning.

Violating Expectations

In the late 1970s, researcher Judee Burgoon explained how violations of our expectations trigger attention.[1] The word *violations* in this context doesn't necessarily imply something negative. When Jeanette took her car in to have the tires rotated, they did that and also changed the oil by accident. Explaining what they had done, they assured her it would be no extra charge since it was their mistake. Jeanette offered to pay, since an oil change had been coming due anyway, but they flatly refused. This action by the auto shop constituted a violation of Jeanette's expectations. It was not what she expected to happen, but she deeply appreciated it, and obviously I'm still talking about it today. For good as well as bad, breaking people's expectations triggers their attention and sticks in their memories.

If a storyteller always uses suspense or *always* tries to break listener expectations, then these elements would no longer be unexpected, and would have less impact. Effective storytellers know that, if used sparingly, breaking expectations and using suspense can be a highly effective way to tell stories.

Jason Robertson, the pastor of a large church in Ohio, broke expectations to connect profoundly with someone. A woman had been coming to church, largely to drop off her son, yet chose to stay for the worship services while she waited for him. She was a Muslim, and she confronted Jason one Sunday immediately after a service.

"Why are you Christians so arrogant to think you have to evangelize people of other faiths?"

Jason calmly responded, "Do me a favor and promise me you won't come back to a worship service here."

This guy is perhaps the worst evangelical pastor on the planet, right? Who in their right mind would say this to someone?

After an awkward, jaw-dropping silence, Jason continued. "However, we have a group I'm a part of that meets on Saturdays. We prepare meals for the homeless. Come on over. We could use your help cooking. You can ask me questions. We can chat. But don't come back to worship services for a while."

She actually agreed.

It wasn't that he didn't want her in his church; he just knew the worship service would continue to offend her. It was ultimately not what would engage her on her faith journey.

The woman faithfully participated in the Saturday ministry for six months. Then, over the next four years, she became even more involved, was part of a mission trip to Honduras, and even eventually returned to Sunday worship services. On Jason's last Sunday at that church, she was baptized.

Jason explained to me that he now tells this story when explaining how evangelism and discipleship are not separate entities. Many need to see faith lived out and practiced before they accept it. Jason broke expectations with the confrontational woman. She expected a defensive rebuttal, but she received instead something she later said she genuinely appreciated. Jason uses that story to break expectations of listeners for the purpose of teaching about discipleship and evangelism.

Backyard Funeral

In chapter 12, we emphasized the need to adapt our messages to particular audiences. Sometimes a story is the perfect way to give meaning to an otherwise abstract expression like "take up your cross." Michael "ChapDaddy" Benson, a national evangelist for the Priesthood Motorcycle Ministry, accomplishes this with a true story that has an unexpected but powerful ending:

I recently officiated a funeral for a man whom I had never met, nor had I ever met any of his immediate family. The funeral was to begin at two o'clock, or so I was told, and I planned to arrive at noon to meet the family and learn more about the deceased and the family.

I presented myself at the front door around noon. Immediately I was ushered through the house and out the back door to where the family was seated in lounge chairs, all in rows, and facing an old TV tray. On the tray was a coffee can, and inside were the ashes of the deceased. The family was gathered around in five or six rows with others standing behind them.

One of the sons led me straight to the front, where I was handed a service bulletin from the funeral home (that was when I learned the name of the man whose funeral I was conducting!) and introduced as the minister who was there to officiate—apparently, beginning right at that moment. In near shock, I quickly gathered my thoughts and began to address the small crowd of family members and close friends.

After making some appropriate opening remarks, I asked those present if there were any memories they wanted share. Several wanted to make comments about their memories of the deceased. To some he was father; to others, brother or uncle. To many he was friend. To one he was husband. It was as important for us to hear these memories as it was for those who shared them with us. Now the tears were flowing.

Finally a niece said she had an old newspaper editorial she wanted to read. Not being one to stand in the way of family members grieving at a funeral, I gave my okay, and she came to the front to read it to us.

The story was about thirty years old. It was a guest editorial written by an emergency room doctor about an experience he had while on duty one day. A young man had been involved in a serious bicycle accident that caused a compound fracture of his leg—a wound that bled profusely. The victim had been brought to the ER by a taxi driver who was near the scene of the accident. This doctor went to work on the leg. He remarked in the article that the response of the cab driver definitely saved the young man's leg and, perhaps, even his life.

On duty again the next day, the doctor checked in on the patient to see how he was doing and found the young man in tears. The doctor inquired about his pain, but the young man said that wasn't why he was crying. He was crying because the cab was the fifty-ninth car to pass him that day. There were fifty-eight other cars whose drivers slowed down to look at him but drove off rather than stop to help.

"Why did the other fifty-eight cars drive on?" he wanted to know.

At this point in the editorial, the doctor began to shame the readers for their lack of compassion. "This is not one of your big cities like New York or Chicago or Detroit. This is small-town America; Cedar Rapids, Iowa. What's wrong with us?" he wanted to know.

It turns out that the driver of the taxi was the man whose ashes lay in the coffee can in front of me on the TV tray. Here was a man who was not afraid of what it would cost him or overly concerned about the condition of his cab. He simply got busy doing what was in front of him to do.

Crosses are not waiting to be discovered and named "a cross to carry;" rather, they are available to us in the multitude of situations that come across our lives.

ChapDaddy's story represents effective storytelling. It shows adaptation by offering a real story to explain an abstract theological concept. The story connects to our hearts with our human understanding of grief. Although he is a national evangelist and has spoken in elaborate, crowded venues, ChapDaddy keeps it real by choosing a story from a funeral in a backyard. He plays small ball by focusing on just the one concept of carrying the cross. Lastly, he breaks our expectations when we discover at the end that the compassionate taxi driver was the man whose funeral this was. And the story is effective: Through the extraordinary actions of this ordinary man, we are given an image of what it means to find our crosses right in front of us.

A Dilly Bar Resolution

It's not unusual for conflicts to arise in group projects. But this time, things had gotten serious. I had divided my college class into groups of five. Near the end of the semester, I began to receive complaints from members of one particular group. Things eventually got so out of hand that our university's office of Public Safety got involved. The parents of one student threatened to go even further and involve the police because they felt that their child had received threatening text messages and emails from another member of the group. I knew we all had to meet immediately if there was any hope of resolving the conflict before law enforcement was brought in.

I called a mandatory meeting for the group members (sans parents) in my office the next day at two o'clock in the afternoon. One by one, they showed up and took seats on my couch and chairs, which were arranged facing one another. The atmosphere was tense. Once we were all present, I reached behind my desk and opened a cooler. I began to hand out dilly bars. You should have seen the odd looks on their faces as they were forced to hand these around the circle to one another. I opened mine and asked, "So, what's going on?"

The meeting was awkward, difficult, and sometimes tense. But having to actually face one another in the same room was a game changer. Unable to simply zap a spiral of emotionally charged text messages from their rooms, they were forced to sit with and listen to one another. As each member shared his or her side of the story, it became clear that there had been a growing snowball of misunderstandings between two of them in particular. But as we all sat talking, listening, and eating, that snowball began to melt.

Certainly it is not the case that all conflicts can be resolved by simply gathering people together and handing out snacks. But it sure helped this situation, and for a couple reasons. Before having a confrontation in a formal context mediated by a police officer, I wanted to first gather them in a comfortable and neutral context. The dilly bars were also intentionally strategic. I wanted not only to reinforce the informal context, but also to break their expectations. Their situation had escalated to the point that they expected to hear my disappointment, followed by a final judgment and overruling decision. Breaking their expectations by serving them ice cream helped immediately reframe our gathering from a confrontation to a conversation.

Further, their primary context for communication had been through text messages and emails. As we know, these are prone to misunderstanding because they lack the nonverbal cues that are central to communication. Essential body language is absent. Even with an onslaught of emojis, it's nearly impossible to accurately express or understand the emotion that is often central in conflicts. Although online communication was what they had been using and expecting up to this point, what they needed was a face-to-face context. Whether we want to hear a story or tell a story, its message can greatly be affected by context and the breaking of expectations.

And, who doesn't like dilly bars?

Some additional examples could include:

- A pastor begins a message by declaring, "I have given up tithing!" Some members begin to squirm, but everyone is suddenly listening. After an explanation about the church's financial challenges, he shares his enormous gratitude for what the Lord has done in his heart. He then explains that, up until now, he has faithfully given 10 percent of his income. Now, he explains, he has given up tithing, meaning he will no longer give *only* 10 percent of his income. Ten percent will only be a minimum standard. He is committed now to exceeding that amount in response to his enormous gratitude. The initially shocking declaration broke listener's expectations, creating suspense and the response of intent listening.

- The biblical prophet Nathan confronts David's sin with a story of the rich man who took the poor man's ewe lamb. When David's anger demands justice against this rich man, Nathan declares, "You *are* that man." The power of the unexpected message connects with David far more powerfully than if Nathan simply chastised him about his illicit relationship with Bathsheba, before having her husband, Uriah, killed.

- A child comes home from school in tears, having been made fun of for her size. The father's heart breaks for her. He tells her a story from his own childhood. There was a little boy who was heavier than most kids, and one day a bully at recess made fun of him, sending the boy to tears—something that little boy will never forget. The child asks, "You were that little boy, weren't you, Daddy?" "No." The father reveals, "I was the bully." He then comforts his daughter's hurt while challenging her to consider the truth that bullies are often hurting inside themselves, and try to cover up or forget that hurt by causing other people pain.

The Rest of the Story

As I lay on the asphalt parking lot of the Dairy Queen, my brain whirled in hyper speed. *Should I just pretend to be dead? Will my mother see my disturbing crime scene in a newspaper? Is a bullet on its way this very moment?*

I couldn't take the tension. As fast as I could go on my hands and knees, I scrambled toward a parked car, where I could take cover. Before I reached it, however, the sound of gunfire was replaced with that of squealing tires.

The scene was again quiet. Eventually Chris and other patrons popped up like prairie dogs from inside the store, peering out the windows.

Sirens.

Police reports. Trembling, I offered useless descriptions: *It was a guy. He had a gun. He was wearing an army jacket. Or was it a denim jacket?*

In the midst of those surreal moments, I noticed something in my hand—my Blizzard and spoon. Despite the diving, rolling, and crawling that had torn up my knees and elbows, I hadn't let go of my ice cream. As we drove home in the darkness, I finished every bite. And as Paul Harvey would say, now you know...the rest of the story!

Reflect or Discuss

1. The author writes that, "for good as well as bad, breaking people's expectations triggers their attention and sticks in their memories." What are some stories you remember because of how the storytellers broke your expectations while telling them?

2. Jason Robertson broke the expectations of the Muslim woman by not responding with defensiveness or argument. Why do you suppose his particular response proved to be more effective?

3. Why would ChapDaddy's funeral story have been weaker had he begun by telling us that the funeral was for a former taxi driver? How does that unexpected ending add power to his simple conclusion about what it means to carry the cross? How did his other details of the situation and setting surrounding the funeral itself contribute to the effectiveness of his story?

4. Breaking expectations begins with knowing what a listener (or audience) expects from us. What do they expect you to say? How do they expect you to say it? How might breaking those expectations keep their attention and make your message more memorable when speaking with:
   a. Your children, spouse, parents, etc.?
   b. Your church, those you spiritually mentor, or those who are mentoring you?
   c. Those with whom you work?
   d. Your neighbors and friends?

18   Use Sensory Aids

The Faded Map

"Let's meet for coffee; we'll talk," I said in a text message to my son. T.J. accepted my offer, and the next morning we each drove half-way and met at a coffee shop. He was discouraged. He had received a rejection letter from his first choice of schools for doctoral studies. For a young man to whom so much success had come, the rejection letter felt like failure. That feeling of failure led to his fear: *What if everything I've worked for suddenly stops here?* Between bites of his cinnamon scone, he shared. He still had other applications out there, but he was growing increasingly fearful of their statuses.

I listened. Then I slid three faded sheets of paper across the table. Two featured a hand-drawn table of rows and columns. It was a table—of seventy-eight universities to which I had applied back in 1993—that allowed me to track where I had sent my résumé, who still needed letters of recommendation, and more. Some of the applications had been sent to schools that had posted open positions; others were unsolicited. The third sheet was a photocopied map of the United States with seventy-eight hand-drawn red dots in cities ranging from coast to coast.

"These," I explained, "represent the schools where I applied." He gazed at the map, and I continued, "But look again at the list of schools on this other sheet. Notice that all but two are crossed out with a red pen—my rejection letters. Having only two possibilities out of seventy-eight was discouraging. Now look back at the map. All but two of these dots represent rejection. But also notice there's no dot in Bourbonnais, Illinois." Of course, T.J. knew that Bourbonnais is the home of Olivet Nazarene University, where I teach. "I didn't even bother applying to my alma mater because I knew they didn't have an opening. Yet, out of the blue one evening, I received a call from their communications department chairman, Dr. David Kale. He himself was leaving, which meant they had an opening—and they wanted me."

I then reminded T.J. about when Samuel holds interviews in the Bible with the sons of Jesse to see which one God will anoint as the next king of Israel. One by one, seven are reviewed by Samuel, and each has strong qualities, but none is the one whom the Lord wants. So who gets the job? The one who hasn't even applied! Jesse's youngest son, David, is summoned from the field, and Samuel knows immediately that David is to be God's chosen leader.

"On paper," I explained, holding the map and list, "things can look discouraging. But God has a plan. And God knows where you are, and God can do whatever he needs to do to find you and lead you to where you need to be."

T.J. needed a challenge story to encourage him. Meeting him the very morning after he received his bad news impacted the message of my challenge story through the use of context. He needed to hear it immediately (timing) and, ideally, face to face in our favorite environment, a coffee shop (place/space). But to help make the message stick, I wanted a visual image to reinforce the story. The image I chose was the actual map I had kept in a file for more than two decades. It was something tangible to hand him. All the dots and crossed-off university names visually told the story: *I empathize with your rejection and discouragement.* In addition, the second story of David's selection reinforced the lesson the Lord had taught me: *Have faith because he is faithful.*

Olm Sweet Olm

Imagine living your entire life in a cave—and not just any cave, but an underwater cave, in total darkness. What would you need to survive there? At a minimum, you would need the human essentials of ramen noodles and reliable WiFi (obviously!). The olm, a type of salamander, sadly has neither of these instruments of basic survival. Oh, and it also doesn't have eyes. Living in total darkness for up to fifty years, it doesn't need them. Instead, this little guy, who reaches nearly a foot long, relies on hearing and smell to find food consisting of worms, larvae, and snails. With nothing to see in total darkness, these other senses are all he needs to feel right at olm—I mean, *home*—in the cave.

Humans, obviously, are not olms. Although statistics vary and they claim these are estimates at best, the National Federation of the Blind suggests that, as of 2012, anywhere between 1.2 percent and 3.9 percent of adults in the United States were visually impaired.[1] Thankfully, many of these individuals have learned to rely on other senses. For the remaining 96 to 98 percent of us, however, sight remains a critical way that we perceive information, but we also perceive information through hearing, smell, touch, and taste. These senses provide us with numerous ways of experiencing life, taking in information, and learning.

Good teachers know this. Not all of us learn the same way. Some learn by listening to an effective lecture. Others learn visually. Still others learn best through hands-on experience. If we can learn something through a combination of senses, it becomes connected (remember the burdock analogy?) in our minds more firmly.

I had to do a how-to demonstration in my high school speech class. I chose How to Make a Blueberry Pie. I explained it verbally, put it together in front of them, and handed out samples, effectively utilizing all five senses. The more senses we can utilize in sharing our stories, the greater potential there is for these stories to become embedded in the minds and memories of our listeners. We often hear of the value of using visual aids, but these only account for one sense. While that sense is critical, we need to consider more broadly the use of sensory aids. Once we know the message we want to communicate, we simply ask ourselves which sensory aids could best reinforce it for our listeners. For my message to my son, it was sight and touch as I handed him the map and my list of rejections.

Someone who has mastered the art of using sensory aids to reinforce his storytelling is Dr. Leon Blanchette, a theology professor at Olivet who leads children's church at Kankakee First Church of the Nazarene in Illinois. When he teaches children about Passover, he has them sit on the floor in circles of about five each. In front of each child sits a plate of unusual foods—each representing parts of a traditional Seder meal. He explains what each item on their plates symbolizes for the Jews, during which the children get to taste the food. They eat a bit of horseradish on matzo as he explains the bitterness of Israel's slavery and the bitterness of sin. Each of their senses is fully utilized in this activity. As a result, their understanding of the story behind the Seder meal is deeply embedded in their minds and hearts.

When I asked him why he does things like this, Dr. Blanchette said:

I love to tell stories. I believe God created humans as story-formed people. In my opinion, one of the most effective ways to support storytelling is through the use of sensory aids. In a children's worship service, not only are stories being told, but the entire service is one continuing story of worship. The lighting of a candle, the kneeling at altars for prayer, the creative activity that follows the story, are all sensory aids in the telling of the greater story—the reason we are present, worship. Sensory aids provide opportunities for children to personalize the stories they are hearing so they not only know the story but, more importantly, may be transformed by the story. Storytelling and sensory aids are two sides of the same coin.

Synecdoches and Symbols

As the civil unrest grows, will the president commit U.S. boots to the ground?

I know you're tempted, but don't risk losing your three-month chip.

Here I raise my Ebenezer.

Boots, chips, and any number of items representing Ebenezers are all symbols of significantly larger concepts. These function as synecdoches (pronounced sihn-ECT-uh-keys); they are each a small part representing a larger whole. Boots represent American troops. Chips represent benchmarks of sobriety for recovering alcoholics. Ebenezers are symbols unique to believers that represent a place or moment of major commitment to the Lord. Whether as rhetorical devices (e.g., boots on the ground) or as physical objects we keep (e.g., chips), these are powerful symbols. They are not merely metaphors and trinkets; for us, they become the embodiment of our stories.

Sensory items of multiple kinds can function symbolically to evoke stories. Many of her friends think of Jeanette whenever they smell her perfume—the only one she has used for many years. Our sense of smell can take us back to childhood memories, both good and bad: fresh-cut grass, cookies in the oven, cigar smoke, freshly fertilized fields, or hospitals. A song can immediately trigger a specific day and time from many years ago. Odd lots of things are kept in wooden boxes strung with silver wire, plastic bins in the attic, or bedside tables. Macaroni crafts and construction paper drawings of stick figures and smiling suns adorn our shelves. They may be tossed out when we're gone, but while we are alive, they serve as story stimulators.

As storied leaders, we want to tell our stories well. Given that we experience the world through five senses, let's use as many of them as possible. Naturally, our choice of sensory aids will depend on multiple factors related to our audience and context: demographic factors, available media, and the availability of the particular sensory aids desired. Our choices should always be driven by the message we want to send and the needs of the particular listener or audience. The bottom line, however, is that sensory aids provide additional channels through which to express and reinforce a single message. If I can find additional ways of connecting an important idea for a listener, why wouldn't I invest the time and effort to do so? The later memory of the object, image, video, or music I use may stimulate association with my story's message.

Some additional examples could include:

- Showing your son a faded photograph of his great-grandmother when explaining the legacy of faith that she left as a prayer warrior.
- After leading a group of young college men on a rock-climbing and mission trip in California, the co-leader and I held a small ceremony for them. We asked them to get dressed up and meet in a small chapel. Together we committed to being men of God, marking it with machetes engraved with their names and the words of Proverbs 27:17: "As iron sharpens iron, so one person sharpens another."
- A pastor using a variety of creative sensory aids (showing an object as part of an analogy, playing a short video, organizing a live dramatic sketch, or using key visual imagery or text on slides) during a sermon that make the message more memorable. These are most powerful if used in variety for the purpose of breaking expectations.

Dr. Blanchette shares a few additional examples of sensory aids he uses in children's worship on a fairly regular basis:

- A candle is lit at the beginning of each worship service as a reminder of God's presence among us in the service. When the candle is extinguished at the end of the service, it serves as a reminder that God does not live in the building but in our hearts; therefore, he leaves with us.
- At the end of small group sharing time, students are released to a number of centers that contain art-and-craft-type activities that students may use to relive the story. These items include individual dry-erase boards, Play-Doh, Legos, Lincoln Logs, journals, or blocks. All of these sensory items are intended to allow the students to live in the story through their own imaginations.
- Creative pictures are used during the service to teach a particular book of the Bible and a main theme of the book. These are done in chronological order so children learn the books of the Bible in order and a key thought about each book. The pictures tend to implant in children's long-term memories, and often children can remember the themes of books years after they have been taught.

- Simple drawings of pictures that connect to major stories of the Bible are used as a way to remember the key stories of the meta-narrative of Scripture. For example, a picture of the earth for the story of creation, a campfire for the story of Isaac, a coat for the story of Joseph, a lamb for Passover.

- A simple object is often used as a visual during the telling of a story (biblical or nonbiblical). For example, a shoebox was used to tell a story of how a gift through Operation Christmas Child made a significant difference in the life of a particular child.

- During the Advent season, items are used to teach important truths connected to the season. A candy cane is used to teach the legend of the candy cane. *Crismons* are Christmas decorations in the shape of church icons—a cross, alpha and omega, crown, etc. Prior to several items being placed on the tree during each of the four weeks of Advent, an explanation of the significance of each symbol is explained.

While our choice of sensory aids can be as complex as an original dramatic sketch or short video, they certainly don't have to be. Jesus drew in the sand, pointed to a fig tree, and drew attention to the image of Caesar on the back of a coin. We too can reinforce our stories with photos, simple objects, music, items from nature, small gifts, and even food. As storied leaders, let's maximize our influence by connecting our messages to listeners through their five senses.

Reflect or Discuss

1. Recall two or three items that may hold very little material value yet serve as powerful story stimulators for you. How did those stories become attached to these items?

2. What types of sensory aids are particularly effective at connecting stories to your memory? Objects? Videos? Music? Graphics? Pictures? Smells? Tastes? Identify an example of someone whose story you recall because the storyteller utilized one of these sensory aids effectively.

3. Although some of us are tempted to prefer the use of one type of sensory aid over another (some are comfortable using PowerPoint slides, others with the use of video clips), how does effective communication depend instead upon picking the sensory aid(s) most likely to appeal to our listeners or audience?

4. Remember Corey MacPherson's story from chapter 13, in which he asked students to send him photos illustrating what grace meant to them? One girl submitted a photo of her brother with cerebral palsy, accompanied by her short explanation. How did the inclusion of the photo make her story of grace so much more powerful?

5. The author reminds us that sensory aids don't have to be complicated or expensive. What readily available and free sensory aids do you have that could help you tell:
   a. An identity story about your church or ministry?
   b. A vision story for your church or ministry?
   c. A challenge story to a discouraged friend or family member?
   d. A counter story to correct a misperception about your church, ministry, or faith?
   e. A change story to someone who needs to be inspired and motivated toward change?

Conclusion

What did you do today? I'll bet it has already involved stories. You may have begun your day reading, watching, or listening to news stories. You may have read a devotional story. You probably opened your email and read stories: advertisements, complaints, problems that need your attention, updates, and the crazy stories from that one particular friend whose emails you always open first. You probably received some quick stories sent through text or social media messages. At work you heard and told stories. Your spouse, children, and friends told you stories about their days. You may have entertained yourself with stories via television and movies. When you gather with friends, yes, that's right, more stories. The day you were born, your parents told you stories about who you were and how they loved you. At your funeral, your children will do the same. Friends—*we live storied lives!*

The earliest to most recently recorded stories reveal our human fascination with the journey narrative. Within the pages or screens, we identify with the protagonist—often an ordinary person who ventures out of her status quo (by force or choice). Facing some conflict, she seeks resolution. Often aided by one or more along her path, her journey culminates with a life-transforming encounter with something larger than herself. This results in a forever-changed future. This is the story we as humans have been telling over and over and over.

The reason this core narrative is so central is that this is how God designed us. He wants us to recognize our incompleteness to drive us toward him—the only one capable of saving and transforming us. Although we all relate to the narrative life pattern of seeking resolution for our struggles, many seek resolution through people and things unable to provide it. We can provide assistance to others on their journeys seeking the Hero.

Ever watch a movie and find yourself saying, "That's not realistic"? The story doesn't quite add up? Even when you know it's fiction, you want it to have a sense of narrative fidelity or plausibility. Worse is when this happens in our own lives. Sometimes our words and stories give testimony to Christ's transformative power, but our actions and lives suggest a contrary story. Our words and actions don't line up. Nothing kills the power of a Christian's story faster than having this sense of narrative infidelity, or what amounts to hypocrisy. Our testimony for Christ is then akin to plagiarism, copied and spoken but not authentic and real to the speaker.

More important than becoming a better storyteller is getting the story straight. If you're living a plagiarized testimony—real to someone else but not to yourself, stop leading. Get your story straight. Christ wants to write his story of transformation in your life. Then—and only then—become a storied leader and tell it.

Further, as you experience the daily, routine stuff of life, look for new stories. They're everywhere. The Lord has even taught me valuable lessons from my observations of my dog. She's a greyhound, bred and built for one thing: running. But when I took her jogging with me one day, I found myself nearly dragging her along behind me. And trust me, I'm extremely slow. I suddenly had this image of how this must look to God when I fail to use the gifts and abilities he has bestowed in me—what a waste! I need to use my strengths for his glory. You might not have a dog (although, if you want one, I've got a lazy greyhound for you!). For you, it may be things you observe at work, at home with your children, in life as an aunt, as a grandparent, as a Sunday school teacher, or while working retail. Look for stories, asking yourself how they might be used to encourage someone someday. Mentally stash them away. The story closet of your brain should be overflowing. Look, you've got pants in your closet that you will never fit into again; give them away to charity. But you *will* someday use your stories—even years from now—when the time calls for them.

Don't throw anything away, but for heaven's sake, please organize your stories. One way to do this is to ask yourself the common types of dissonance you encounter. For instance, do you seem to run across people whose source of dissonance is hypocrisy? Or is it their complaint against organized religion? Or is it the difficulty of exercising faith? Do people struggle with the notion of tithing? Whatever these main points of dissonance are that you seem to encounter, locate stories for them. In other words, what is a good analogy (one that really makes sense to you personally) that helps offer insight into that problem? Do people you meet tend to have difficulty understanding theological terms (the grammar of faith)? Ask yourself what examples you have that best illustrate grace, forgiveness, sanctification, and so on. You might think of a story on the spot, but it's better if you've already thought of some examples to use in these situations. Since they are your own stories, there's no trouble memorizing them. You already know them. Just learn to tell them well.

Use the power of narrative to encourage others toward stronger relationships with Christ. Be a storyteller. But you are not only a storyteller; *you are also a story.* What will be your own narrative legacy? What stories will people tell about you when you are gone? Hopefully they'll be kind, flattering, and even funny. But will they refer to you as a leader? Many of us don't particularly view ourselves as leaders. Politicians are leaders. Bosses are leaders. Clergy and church officials are leaders. True, they are. But so are you. Remember our definition of leadership: the intentional act of guiding or influencing others for their well-being. If this sounds like you, then you are a leader.

Develop your leadership through prayer, study, practice, and learning from other leaders. But some of your best opportunities to connect with and lead others will begin with sharing stories of what Christ has done in your own life. Lead as the person God created you to be. This will become your own narrative legacy, when you are no longer the story*teller* but, rather, the story *told.*

Notes

Introduction

1. Fred B. Craddock, *Craddock on the Craft of Preaching*. Edited by Lee Sparks and Kathryn Hayes Sparks (St. Louis: Chalice Press, 2011), 24.

Chapter 2

1. Richard L. Johannesen, Rennard Strickland, and Ralph T. Eubanks, editors. *Language Is Sermonic: Richard M. Weaver on the Nature of Rhetoric* (Baton Rouge: Louisiana State University Press, 1970), 225.

2. John Leland Peters, *Christian Perfection and American Methodism* (New York: Abingdon Press, 1956), 31.

3. Walter Houston Clark, *The Psychology of Religion: An Introduction to Religious Experience and Behavior* (New York: Macmillan, 1958), 195.

Chapter 3

1. Joseph Campbell, *The Hero with a Thousand Faces*. Third Edition (Novato, CA: New World Library, 2008).

Chapter 4

1. Bill Hybels, *Just Walk Across the Room: Simple Steps Pointing People to Faith* (Grand Rapids: Zondervan, 2006), 120–21.

Chapter 5

1. *http://brecheen.org/cbrecheen/WhatImGivingYouForChristmas.htm*. Last accessed March 8, 2016.

2. Craddock, *Craft of Preaching*, 25.

3. Paul Ekman and Wallace V. Friesen, "Nonverbal Leakage and Clues to Deception," *Journal for the Study of Interpersonal Processes*, Vol. 32, 1968, 88–106.

4. Paul Ekman and Wallace V. Friesen, "The Repertoire of Nonverbal Behavior: Categories, Origins, Usage, and Coding," *Semiotica*, Vol. 1, 1969, 49–98.

Chapter 6

1. Leon Festinger, *A Theory of Cognitive Dissonance* (Stanford, CA: Stanford University Press, 1957).

2. Douglas Stone, Bruce M. Patton, and Sheila Heen, *Difficult Conversations: How to Discuss What Matters Most* (New York: Penguin Books, 2010).

Chapter 7

1. *http://www.elwoodstaffing.com.* Last accessed March 8, 2016.

Chapter 8

1. John C. Bowling, *ReVision: 13 Strategies to Renew Your Work, Your Organization, and Your Life* (Kansas City: Beacon Hill Press of Kansas City, 2013), 89–90.

2. *http://www.turlockjournal.com/archives/5025.* Last accessed March 8, 2016.

Chapter 9

1. Stephen Denning, *The Leader's Guide to Storytelling: Mastering the Art and Discipline of Business Narrative* (San Francisco: Jossey-Bass, 2011), 217.

2. James L. Golden, Goodwin Fauntleroy Berquist, William E. Coleman, and J. Michael Sproule, *The Rhetoric of Western Thought: From the Mediterranean World to the Global Setting.* Tenth Edition (Dubuque, IA: Kendall Hunt Publishing, 2011), 83.

Chapter 10

1. *http://www.americanrhetoric.com/speeches/mlkihaveadream.htm.* Last accessed March 8, 2016.

Chapter 11

1. Craddock, *Craft of Preaching*, 33.

2. Denning, *Leader's Guide to Storytelling*, 72.

Section IV

1. Chip Heath and Dan Heath, *Made to Stick: Why Some Ideas Survive and Others Die* (New York: Random House, 2008), 19.

Chapter 12

1. Stan Toler, *The Inspirational Speaker's Resource: Tools for Reaching Your Audience Every Time* (Kansas City: Beacon Hill Press of Kansas City, 2009).

2. Kevin B. Zook, "Teaching and Learning by Analogy: Psychological Perspectives on the Parables of Jesus," *ICCTE Journal*, Vol. 6, Issue 1, January 2009. *http://icctejournal.org.*

Chapter 13

1. Chip Heath and Dan Heath. *Switch: How to Change Things When Change Is Hard* (New York: Crown Publishing, 2010), 7.

2. *http://www.pbs.org/now/shows/526/homeless-facts.html.* Last accessed March 8, 2016.

3. *http://homeless.samhsa.gov/resourcefiles/hrc_factsheet.pdf.* Last accessed March 8, 2016.

Chapter 14

1. Erving Goffman, *The Presentation of Self in Everyday Life* (Garden City, NY: Doubleday Anchor Books, 1959).

2. William Shakespeare, *As You Like It*, Act II, Scene VII.

Chapter 16

1. Jan De Houwer, Sarah Thomas, and Frank Bayens, "Associative Learning of Likes and Dislikes: A Review of 25 Years of Research on Human Evaluative Conditioning," *Psychological Bulletin*, Vol. 127, 2001, 853–69.

2. Gordon Bower, Kenneth Monteiro, and Stephen Gilligan, "Emotional Mood for Learning and Recall," *Journal of Verbal Learning and Verbal Behavior*, Vol. 17, 1978, 573–85.

3. Donna Bridge, Joan Chiao, and Ken Paller, "Emotional Context at Learning Systematically Biased Memory for Facial Information," *Memory and Cognition*, Vol. 38(2), 2010, 125–33.

Chapter 17

1. Judee Burgoon, "Nonverbal Violations of Expectations." John Wiemann and Randall Harrison (Eds.), *Nonverbal Interaction* (Beverly Hills: Sage, 1983), 11–77.

Chapter 18

1. *https://nfb.org/blindness-statistics.* Last accessed March 8, 2016.